Fun Math Problem Solving
For Elementary School
Volume 2

Areteem Institute

TITLES PUBLISHED BY ARETEEM PRESS

Cracking the High School Math Competitions (and Solutions Manual) - Covering AMC 10 & 12, ARML, and ZIML

Mathematical Wisdom in Everyday Life (and Solutions Manual) - From Common Core to Math Competitions

Geometry Problem Solving for Middle School (and Solutions Manual) - From Common Core to Math Competitions

Fun Math Problem Solving For Elementary School (and Solutions Manual)

Fun Math Problem Solving For Elementary School Vol. 2

ZIML MATH COMPETITION BOOK SERIES

ZIML Math Competition Book Division E 2016-2017
ZIML Math Competition Book Division M 2016-2017
ZIML Math Competition Book Division H 2016-2017
ZIML Math Competition Book Jr Varsity 2016-2017
ZIML Math Competition Book Varsity Division 2016-2017
ZIML Math Competition Book Division E 2017-2018
ZIML Math Competition Book Division M 2017-2018
ZIML Math Competition Book Division H 2017-2018
ZIML Math Competition Book Jr Varsity 2017-2018
ZIML Math Competition Book Varsity Division 2017-2018
ZIML Math Competition Book Division E 2018-2019
ZIML Math Competition Book Division M 2018-2019
ZIML Math Competition Book Division H 2018-2019
ZIML Math Competition Book Jr Varsity 2018-2019
ZIML Math Competition Book Varsity Division 2018-2019

MATH CHALLENGE CURRICULUM TEXTBOOKS SERIES

Math Challenge I-A Pre-Algebra and Word Problems
Math Challenge I-B Pre-Algebra and Word Problems
Math Challenge I-C Algebra
Math Challenge II-A Algebra
Math Challenge II-B Algebra
Math Challenge III Algebra
Math Challenge I-A Geometry
Math Challenge I-B Geometry
Math Challenge I-C Topics in Algebra

Math Challenge II-A Geometry
Math Challenge II-B Geometry
Math Challenge III Geometry
Math Challenge I-A Counting and Probability
Math Challenge I-B Counting and Probability
Math Challenge I-C Geometry
Math Challenge II-A Combinatorics
Math Challenge II-B Combinatorics
Math Challenge III Combinatorics
Math Challenge I-A Number Theory
Math Challenge I-B Number Theory
Math Challenge I-C Finite Math
Math Challenge II-A Number Theory
Math Challenge II-B Number Theory
Math Challenge III Number Theory

COMING SOON FROM ARETEEM PRESS

Fun Math Problem Solving For Elementary School Vol. 2 Solutions Manual
Counting & Probability for Middle School (and Solutions Manual) - From Common Core to Math Competitions
Number Theory Problem Solving for Middle School (and Solutions Manual) - From Common Core to Math Competitions

The books are available in paperback and eBook formats (including Kindle and other formats).
To order the books, visit https://areteem.org/bookstore.

Fun Math Problem Solving For Elementary School Vol. 2

Edited by   David Reynoso
             John Lensmire
             Kevin Wang
             Kelly Ren

ISBN-10: 1-944863-49-4
ISBN-13: 978-1-944863-49-4

First printing, May 2020.

Contents

Introduction

This book is the continuation of the book titled "Fun Math Problem Solving For Elementary School" (that book can be regarded as "Volume 1" of the series), as part of the ongoing effort by Areteem Institute to inspire students, parents, and teachers to gain a deeper understanding and appreciation of mathematics. This book series is aimed for students in 3rd, 4th, and 5th grade in elementary school. This book reviews and expands state math standards, including the Common Core Standards, particularly the Operations and Algebraic Thinking (OA), Numbers and Operations in Base Ten (NBT), and Measurement and Data (MD) domains at the 3rd, 4th, and 5th grade level.

The book is divided into 8 chapters. Similar to Volume 1, in each of the chapters we introduce a new concept as well as step by step solutions to a variety of problems related to that particular concept. Each chapter contains 10 example questions with full solutions, 10 quick response questions and 25 practice problems. The problems are designed to test the students' mastery of the material discussed in each chapter.

The book is available as a Student Workbook and has an accompanying Solutions Manual with full solutions. The Student Workbook contains all the material and practice problems, and answers to all practice problems. The Solutions Manual includes in-depth solutions to all of the quick response and practice problems.

The problems in this book offer the student a chance to start developing problem solving techniques that will be useful not only in mathematics but also in everyday life.

Common Core and This Book

Teachers and students working in 3rd, 4th, and 5th grade math can use this book to teach and learn mathematical reasoning and problem solving, focusing on concepts in the OA (Operations and Algebraic Thinking), NBT (Numbers and Operations in Base Ten), Numbers and Operations-Fractions (NF), and MD (Measurement and Data) Common Core domains.

For reference, a summary of these domains is provided below.

Operations and Algebraic Thinking	
Standard(s)	Cluster
3.OA.1-4	Represent and solve problems involving multiplication and division.
3.OA.5-6	Understand properties of multiplication and the relationship between multiplication and division.
3.OA.7	Multiply and divide within 100.
3.OA.8-9	Solve problems involving the four operations, and identify and explain patterns in arithmetic.
4.OA.1-3	Use the four operations with whole numbers to solve problems.
4.OA.4	Gain familiarity with factors and multiples.
4.OA.5	Generate and analyze patterns.
5.OA.1-2	Write and interpret numerical expressions.
5.OA.3	Analyze patterns and Relationships.

Numbers and Operations in Base Ten	
Standard(s)	Cluster
3.NBT.1-3	Use place value understanding and properties of operations to perform multi-digit arithmetic.
4.NBT.1-3	Generalize place value understanding for multi-digit whole numbers.
4.NBT.4-6	Use place value understanding and properties of operations to perform multi-digit arithmetic.
5.NBT.1-4	Understand the place value system.
5.NBT.5-7	Perform operations with multi-digit whole numbers and with decimals to hundredths.

Numbers and Operations-Fractions	
Standard(s)	Cluster
3.NF.1-3	Develop understanding of fractions as numbers.
4.NF.1-2	Extend understanding of fraction equivalence and ordering.
4.NF.3-4	Build fractions from unit fractions by applying and extending previous understandings of operations on whole numbers.
4.NF.5-7	Understand decimal notation for fractions, and compare decimal fractions.
5.NF.1-2	Use equivalent fractions as a strategy to add and subtract fractions.
5.NF.3-7	Apply and extend previous understandings of multiplication and division to multiply and divide fractions.

Measurement and Data	
Standard(s)	Cluster
3.MD.1-2	Solve problems involving measurement and estimation of intervals of time, liquid volumes, and masses of objects.
3.MD.3-4	Represent and interpret data.
3.MD.5-7	Geometric measurement: understand concepts of area and relate area to multiplication and to addition.
3.MD.8	Geometric measurement: recognize perimeter as an attribute of plane figures and distinguish between linear and area measures.
4.MD.1-3	Solve problems involving measurement and conversion of measurements from a larger unit to a smaller unit.
4.MD.4	Represent and interpret data.
4.MD.5-7	Geometric measurement: understand concepts of angle and measure angles.
5.MD.1	Convert like measurement units within a given measurement system.
5.MD.2	Represent and interpret data.
5.MD.3-5	Geometric measurement: understand concepts of volume and relate volume to multiplication and to addition.

The start of each chapter summarizes the specific Common Core standards emphasized in the chapter. In addition, the problem solving stressed in the exercises allows students to practice the other standards simultaneously, even if those standards are not the focus of the chapter.

For more details about the specific standards, clusters, and domains quoted above, see `www.corestandards.org/Math` where the full Mathematical Standards are available for download.

About Areteem Institute

Areteem Institute is an educational institution that develops and provides in-depth and advanced math and science programs for K-12 (Elementary School, Middle School, and High School) students and teachers. Areteem programs are accredited supplementary programs by the Western Association of Schools and Colleges (WASC). Students may attend the Areteem Institute in one or more of the following options:

- Live and real-time face-to-face online classes with audio, video, interactive online whiteboard, and text chatting capabilities;
- Self-paced classes by watching the recordings of the live classes;
- Short video courses for trending math, science, technology, engineering, English, and social studies topics;
- Summer Intensive Camps held on prestigious university campuses and Winter Boot Camps;
- Practice with selected free daily problems and monthly ZIML competitions at ziml.areteem.org.

Areteem courses are designed and developed by educational experts and industry professionals to bring real world applications into STEM education. The programs are ideal for students who wish to build their mathematical strength in order to excel academically and eventually win in Math Competitions (AMC, AIME, USAMO, IMO, ARML, MathCounts, Math Olympiad, ZIML, and other math leagues and tournaments, etc.), Science Fairs (County Science Fairs, State Science Fairs, national programs like Intel Science and Engineering Fair, etc.) and Science Olympiads, or for students who purely want to enrich their academic lives by taking more challenging courses and developing outstanding analytical, logical, and creative problem solving skills.

Since 2004 Areteem Institute has been teaching with methodology that is highly promoted by the new Common Core State Standards: stressing the conceptual level understanding of the math concepts, problem solving techniques, and solving problems with real world applications. With the guidance from experienced and passionate professors, students are motivated to explore concepts deeper by identifying an interesting problem, researching it, analyzing it, and using a critical thinking approach to come up with multiple solutions.

Thousands of math students who have been trained at Areteem have achieved top honors and earned top awards in major national and international math competitions, including Gold Medalists in the International Math Olympiad (IMO), top winners and qualifiers at the USA Math Olympiad (USAMO/JMO) and AIME, top winners at the

Zoom International Math League (ZIML), and top winners at the MathCounts National Competition. Many Areteem Alumni have graduated from high school and gone on to enter their dream colleges such as MIT, Cal Tech, Harvard, Stanford, Yale, Princeton, U Penn, Harvey Mudd College, UC Berkeley, or UCLA. Those who have graduated from colleges are now playing important roles in their fields of endeavor.

Further information about Areteem Institute, as well as updates and errata of this book, can be found online at http://www.areteem.org.

Acknowledgments

This book contains many years of collaborative work by the staff of Areteem Institute. This book could not have existed without their efforts. The materials in this book were prepared by Kelly Ren and Kevin Wang for Areteem's Young Math Olympians courses, and were later updated and expanded by John Lensmire and David Reynoso. Especially, the illustrations in each chapter were created by David. Yes, the same David Reynoso who is a mathematician by trade and artist by nature!

The examples and problems in this book were either created by the Areteem staff or adapted from various sources, including other books and online resources. We extend our gratitude to the original authors of all these resources.

Last but not least, special thanks go to Saber and Hazel, who starred in the pictures on the covers and chapter images, photographed by Kelly Ren.

1. Prime Chocolates

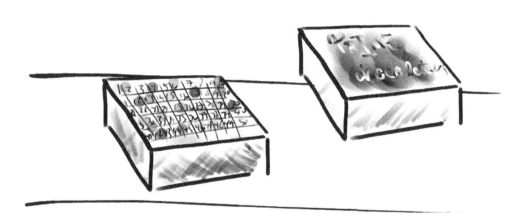

Javier bought a box of *Prime Chocolates*. The box came with 50 chocolates arranged in 5 rows of 10 chocolates each. The chocolates were numbered 1 to 50 and the box came with instructions to *reveal* the *Prime Chocolates*:

1. Eat the first chocolate.
2. Look at the chocolate number 2. *Don't eat it!* Instead, jump 2 spaces and eat chocolate number 4, then jump 2 spaces again and eat number 6, and so on, until all even numbered chocolates (except 2) are eaten.

3. Find the chocolate with the next smallest number after 2, which is now 3. *Again, don't eat it.* Jump 3 spaces to get to number 6. Number 6 is already eaten, so jump 3 spaces again to number 9 and eat it. Keep going until there is no more chocolate to jump to.

4. Keep repeating the above steps: find the next smallest number not yet eaten, and jump ahead with that number of spaces to eat chocolates. Repeat until there are no more chocolate to eat. The chocolates left in the box are the *Prime Chocolates* from this box.

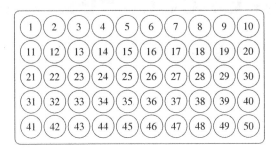

How many *Prime Chocolates* came in Javier's box?

The concepts introduced in this chapter directly correspond to Common Core Math Standards as shown in the following table.

4th Grade	4.OA.4
5th Grade	5.OA.2

In addition to the standards above, problems and concepts in this section will help strengthen understanding of the following domains.

3rd Grade	3.OA
4th Grade	4.OA
5th Grade	5.OA

1.1 Example Questions

Example 1.1

Let's help Javier find all the Prime Chocolates in his box. Remember, Javier has a box with 50 numbered chocolates that came with the following instructions:

1. Eat the first chocolate.
2. Look at the chocolate number 2. *Don't eat it!* Instead, jump 2 spaces and eat chocolate number 4, then jump 2 spaces again and eat number 6, and so on, until all even numbered chocolates (except 2) are eaten.
3. Find the chocolate with the next smallest number after 2, which is now 3. *Again, don't eat it.* Jump 3 spaces to get to number 6. Number 6 is already eaten, so jump 3 spaces again to number 9 and eat it. Keep going until there is no more chocolate to jump to.
4. Keep repeating the above steps: find the next smallest number not yet eaten, and jump ahead with that number of spaces to eat chocolates. Repeat until there are no more chocolate to eat. The chocolates left in the box are the *Prime Chocolates* from this box.

How many Prime Chocolates were there in Javier's box? What numbers were on their labels?

Solution

After Javier ate the first chocolate and all the chocolates with an even label, except for 2, he was left with

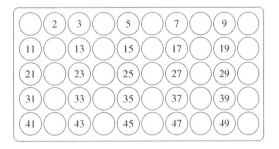

Then after eating all the remaining chocolates with a label that was a multiple of 3, he was left with

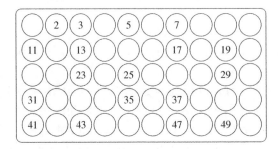

Continuing this way, each time using the newly found Prime Chocolate, Javier's box looked like...

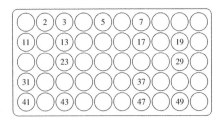
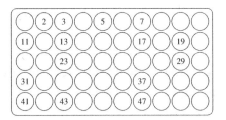

So, there were 15 Prime Chocolates in the box: 2, 3, 5, 7, 11, 13, 17, 19, 23, 29, 31, 37, 41, 43, and 47.

Prime number

All the numbers on the labels of the Prime Chocolates that we helped Javier find are some examples of *prime numbers*.

Remark

The process that Javier followed to eat his chocolates is known as the Sieve of Eratosthenes. In general this process can be used to determine all the prime numbers smaller than certain number (50 in the case of Javier's chocolates).

Example 1.2

Jane got word about the boxes containing Prime Chocolates and got herself a couple of boxes.

She followed the instructions to discover all Prime Chocolates in each of her two boxes, and then she ate the last Prime Chocolate that removed any new chocolates from the box.

What was the Prime Chocolate she ate if her box had

(a) 30 chocolates?

(b) 100 chocolates?

Solution to Part (a)

The first Prime Chocolate, 2, removes all chocolates that have an even number:

$$4, 6, 8, 10, 12, \ldots, 28, 30.$$

The next Prime Chocolate, 3, removes all multiples of 3 that haven't been removed yet; note all even numbers have been removed already, so only odd multiples of 3 remain on the box: $9, 15, 21, 27$.

Prime Chocolate 5 removes all multiples of 5 that have not been removed yet; 10, 15, 20 and 30 have been removed already by 2 and 3, so the first (and only) chocolate that 5 removes is 25.

The next Prime Chocolate, 7, would remove all multiples of 7, but all that were on the box, 14, 21, and 28, have already been removed by 2, 3 and 5, so 7 does not remove any new chocolates. The first chocolate that 7 would remove is $7 \times 7 = 49$, since that is the first multiple of 7 that is not a multiple of 2, 3, or 5, but that number is not in the box.

We can see the same that happened with 7 would happen with all other prime chocolates remaining in the box, so the last Prime Chocolate that removed any chocolates from the box was 5.

Solution to Part (b)

From the previous part we saw that the first Prime Chocolate removed by any Prime Chocolate has a number that is equal to the one of the Prime Chocolate times itself, as we can see in the following table:

Prime Chocolate	Chocolates Removed
2	$4, 6, 8, 10, \ldots, 98, 100$
3	$9, 15, 21, \ldots, 93, 99$
5	$25, 35, 55, \ldots, 85, 95$
7	$49, 77, 91$
11	

Since $11 \times 11 = 121$ is larger than 100, 11 would not remove any new chocolates from the box. Thus Prime Chocolate 7 is the last one to remove any chocolates from the box.

Remark

> When finding all prime numbers smaller than a number n using the Sieve of Eratosthenes, the last prime number p to remove new numbers from the list is the largest prime number such that $p \times p$ is smaller than n.

Example 1.3

Javier had so much fun with his Prime Chocolates that he decided to buy small boxes of Prime Chocolates for all his friends. He bought 12 boxes, each with 10 chocolates.

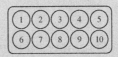

(a) If he gave away every chocolate in every box, how many chocolates did he give away in total?

(b) How many Prime Chocolates did he give away in total?

Solution to Part (a)

Each box has 10 chocolates, thus he gave away $12 \times 10 = 120$ chocolates in total.

Solution to Part (b)

Each small box contains the following Prime Chocolates:

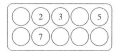

Since each of the boxes contains 4 Prime Chocolates, he gave away $12 \times 4 = 48$ in total.

Multiples

We can find *multiples* of a number if we multiply it by other integers.
In the previous example we can see 120 is a multiple of both 10 and 12, and 48 is a multiple of 4 and 12.

Example 1.4

Jane bought a huge amount of premium truffles and wants to give some away as gifts. Her plan is to give a person 20 premium truffles in a rectangular box.
How many truffles long and how many truffles wide could Jane's rectangular boxes be?

Solution

Note we can write 20 as the product of two numbers, we can do $20 = 4 \times 5$, $20 = 2 \times 10$, or $20 = 1 \times 20$.

So Jane could arrange her truffles in 4 rows of 5 truffles each, 2 rows of 10 truffles, or 1 row of 20 truffles.

Factor

Look at the numbers 1, 2, 4, 5, 10 and 20 in the previous example. For each of them there is another number such that their product is equal to 20, for example, for 4 there is 5, for 2 there is 10, and for 5 there is 4. We call these numbers *factors* of 20.

In general, we say a is a factor of b, if we can write b like a times another (not necessarily different) integer.

Prime number

A prime number is a positive integer that has *exactly two factors*: 1 and itself.

Remark

The number 1 is *not* a prime number! It has only one factor, which is 1 itself. A prime number should have two factors, one is 1, and the other is the prime number itself, which should be different from 1.

Example 1.5

Patrice has a collection of toy soldiers of different colors: green, red, and blue. She wants to make rectangular arrangements with all soldiers in each rectangle being of the same color, and she wants to use all her soldiers so none of them get left out.

How many different rectangular arrangements can she make if she has
  (a) 24 green soldiers?
  (b) 13 red soldiers?
  (c) 58 blue soldiers?

Solution to Part (a)

Patrice will be able to make a different rectangular arrangement for each pair of factors of 24 she can find.

Since

$$24 = 1 \times 24 = 2 \times 12 = 3 \times 8 = 4 \times 6$$

there are 4 different rectangles she could make with her green soldiers.

Solution to Part (b)

13 is a prime number, so its only factors are 1 and 13. This means the only rectangle Patrice can make with her red soldiers is 13 soldiers long and 1 soldier wide.

Solution to Part (c)

The only ways to write 58 as the product of two integers are 1×58 and 2×29, so there are two possible rectangles Patrice could make to arrange her blue soldiers.

Example 1.6

The Prime Chocolate Factory is offering a one time deal to their customers. If a customer sends them the labels of some Prime Chocolates, they will send back a box of Prime Chocolates that contains as many chocolates as the product of all the numbers in the labels that were sent.

(a) Javier wants to get a box of 28 chocolates. Which labels should he send to the Prime Chocolate Factory?

(b) Jane wants to get a box of 36 chocolates. Which labels should she send to the Prime Chocolate Factory?

Solution to Part (a)

To find which labels Javier needs to send, we need to factor the number 28 using only prime numbers. That is, we need to find prime numbers that are equal to 28 when we multiply them all.

To factor a number using only prime numbers it is useful to use a *factor tree*: Start with the number 28 on the top. Since $28 = 4 \times 7$, write 4 and 7 underneath with *branches* connecting them to 28.

Then, since $4 = 2 \times 2$, draw two branches coming out from 4, each of them connecting to a 2.

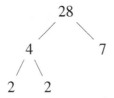

Now all the endings of the tree have prime numbers (2 and 7), so we can say 28 has two different prime factors, 2 and 7, and we can write $28 = 2 \times 2 \times 7$.

Thus, Javier needs to send two labels with the number 2 and one label with the number 7.

Solution to Part (b)

Notice that $36 = 3 \times 12$, $12 = 3 \times 4$, and $4 = 2 \times 2$, which leads to the tree diagram:

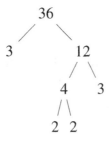

This means 36 has two prime factors: 2 and 3; and

$$36 = 2 \times 2 \times 3 \times 3.$$

Therefore, Jane needs to send two labels with the number 2 and two labels with the number 3.

Remark

Note there may be more than one tree that helps you factor a number. For example these three trees could be used to factor out 36:

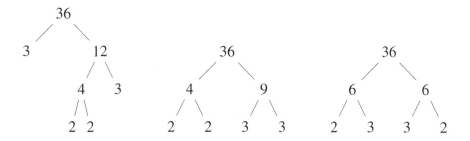

and with all of them we get $36 = 2 \times 2 \times 3 \times 3$.

Example 1.7

Javier decided to buy more boxes of chocolates to share with his whole class. He wants to make sure to give everyone the same number of chocolates and have no leftovers. The boxes of chocolates he found have 14 chocolates each, and there are 16 students in his class (not including him, but he's not giving any chocolates to himself).
What is the least number of boxes of chocolate he is going to need to buy?

Solution

The total number of chocolates that Javier will buy needs to be a multiple of 16, that way he can give everyone the same number of chocolates. The total number of chocolates will also be a multiple of 14, since he is buying whole boxes with 14 chocolates each.

Let's see how many chocolates he would get as he buys more boxes of chocolate:

Number of boxes	1	2	3	4	5	6	7	8	9	10
Number of chocolates	14	28	42	56	70	84	98	112	126	140

We can then compare the total number of chocolates he would need to give in total if he gave 1, 2, 3, etc. chocolates to each of his classmates:

Chocolates per person	1	2	3	4	5	6	7	8	9	10
Number of chocolates	16	32	48	64	80	96	112	128	144	160

Note the smallest number of chocolates that appears on both tables is 112. That corresponds to buying 8 boxes of chocolate and giving 7 chocolates to each student in his class.

Least Common Multiple (LCM)

In the previous example we saw that 112 was the smallest multiple of both 14 and 16, so 112 is the *Least Common Multiple* of 14 and 16.
In general, given two positive integers, the smallest positive integer that is a multiple of both is their *Least Common Multiple* (or *LCM* for short).

Example 1.8

Javier notices that he is eating too many chocolates, so he comes up with a plan to reduce the number of chocolates he eats: He sets up two alarms, one every 24 minutes and one every 42 minutes. He will then eat a chocolate when both alarms go off at the same time.
If he follows through with this plan, how often will Javier get to eat a chocolate?

Solution 1

To find how often will Javier eat a chocolate, we need to find the smallest number of minutes that is a multiple of both 24 and 42, that is, we want to find the LCM of 24 and 42.

To find the LCM of two (or more) numbers, instead of making a list of multiples of each,

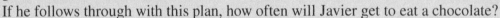

we can use a table to help us out. Start with the numbers to factor on the top, as shown

Then, see if any of the numbers is a multiple of 2. If any of them is, write 2 on the side, and write the quotient of that number divided by 2 below the number itself (if any of the numbers is not divisible by 2, just copy that number down). Repeat the last step until no number is divisible by 2 anymore, then move to the next prime number (3), and so on. Keep repeating these steps until all the numbers have been reduced to 1 (so there will definitely not be any prime factors for any of them anymore). In the case above the table would look like:

	24	42
2	12	21
2	6	21
2	3	21
3	1	7
7		1

Then the LCM of the numbers is the product of all the prime numbers listed on the left side of the table, so the LCM of 24 and 42 is $2 \times 2 \times 2 \times 3 \times 7 = 168$.

This means Javier will get to eat a chocolate every 168 minutes.

Solution 2

Alternatively, we can also factor each of the numbers and look at the prime factors of each of them.

List all the prime factors of each of the numbers and put them side by side. Then for each of the different prime factors, look at which number has the most repetitions. This is how many times this prime factor will be a factor of the LCM of the numbers.

In this case, since $24 = 2 \times 2 \times 2 \times 3$ and $42 = 2 \times 3 \times 7$, we have

24	$2 \times 2 \times 2$	$\times 3$		
42	2		$\times 3$	$\times 7$
LCM	$2 \times 2 \times 2$	$\times 3$	$\times 7$	$= 168$

So the LCM of 24 and 42 is 168.

Example 1.9

Sappy, the frog, is jumping through a row of water lilies with his pal Randy, the toad.

Sappy jumps to every third water lily, and Randy jumps to every fourth lily.

If they are on the same water lily when they start jumping, and always jump at the same time, after how many jumps will Sappy visit a water lily that Randy had already visited?

Solution 1

Number all water lilies in order, starting with 0. Then Sappy visits lilies

$$0, 3, 6, 9, 12, 15, \ldots,$$

and Randy visits lilies

$$0, 4, 8, 12, 16, 20, \ldots.$$

Note the first lily they both visit is the one labeled with the number 12. To get to this lily Sappy needs to jump $12 \div 3 = 4$ times.

Solution 2

Since they jump every third and fourth lily, we can also figure out what is going to be the first lily they both visit by finding the LCM of 3 and 4. Since 3 is a prime number, and $4 = 2 \times 2$, 3 and 4 do not have any factors in common (other than 1), so their LCM is equal to their product $3 \times 4 = 12$.

So Sappy needs to jump $12 \div 3 = 4$ times to get to lily number 12 and Randy needs to jump $12 \div 4 = 3$ times to get to lily number 12.

Note that if they keep jumping they will both visit every twelfth lily, that is, they will both visit lilies $12, 24, 26, 48, 60, \ldots.$

Given two numbers, any common multiple is a multiple of their LCM.

Example 1.10

Jane wants to order some Prime Chocolate boxes. The Factory is having a special sale, where they let you choose one box among 5 boxes, where the 5 boxes contain, respectively, chocolates with numbers 1 to 20, 21 to 40, 41 to 60, 61 to 80, and 81 to 100. The cost of each box is only $2 for each Prime Chocolate it contains. If Jane wants to buy the cheapest box, which one should she buy?

Solution

Using the Sieve of Eratosthenes we can find the prime numbers between 1 and 100. Then we can see which ones are in each of the five boxes to find their price. All of this is summarized in the following table:

Box	Prime Chocolates	Price
$1-20$	$2, 3, 5, 7, 11, 13, 17, 19$	$16
$21-40$	$23, 29, 31, 37$	$8
$41-60$	$41, 43, 47, 53, 59$	$10
$61-80$	$61, 67, 71, 73, 79$	$10
$81-100$	$83, 89, 97$	$6

So the cheapest box is the one with labels $81-100$, since it contains only 3 Prime Chocolates.

Remark

It is a good idea if you write down the prime numbers from 1 to 100.

1.2 Quick Response Questions

Problem 1.1 Find all prime numbers less than 10.

(A) $1, 2, 3, 5$
(B) $2, 3, 5, 7$
(C) $3, 5, 7$
(D) $2, 3, 5$

Problem 1.2 What is the product of the first five prime numbers?

Problem 1.3 What is the prime factorization of 84?

(A) $2 \times 3 \times 11$
(B) $2 \times 3^2 \times 7$
(C) $2 \times 3 \times 7^2$
(D) $2^2 \times 3 \times 7$

Problem 1.4 What are the prime factors of 180?

(A) $2, 3, 5$
(B) $2, 3, 4, 5$
(C) $2, 3, 4, 5, 6$
(D) $1, 2, 3, 4, 5, 6$

Problem 1.5 How many factors does 20 have?

Problem 1.6 What is the sum of the two smallest prime factors of 250?

Problem 1.7 How many distinct prime factors does 56 have?

Problem 1.8 How many factors does 16 have? What are these factors?

(A) 3 factors: $2, 4, 8$
(B) 4 factors: $2, 4, 8, 16$
(C) 5 factors: $1, 2, 4, 8, 16$
(D) 6 factors: $1, 2, 4, 4, 8, 16$

Problem 1.9 Find the LCM of 9 and 12.

Problem 1.10 What is the LCM of 12 and 18?

1.3 Practice

Problem 1.11 How many Prime Chocolates are there in a box with 100 chocolates? What are the labels on these chocolates?

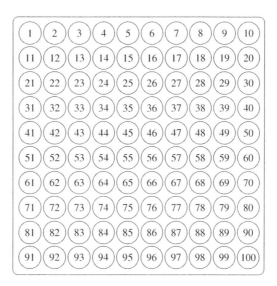

Problem 1.12 Oscar got a box with 100 chocolates labeled 101 to 200. How many of these are Prime Chocolates? What are the labels on these chocolates?

Problem 1.13 List all pairs of numbers whose product equals 36. How many pairs are there?

Problem 1.14 The product of two numbers is 144 and their difference is 10. What is the sum of these numbers?

Problem 1.15 Fill in the blanks

(a) $10 \times \underline{\hspace{1cm}} = 25 \times 4$

(b) $12 \times 5 = 20 \times \underline{\hspace{1cm}}$

(c) $\underline{\hspace{1cm}} \times 6 = 15 \times 20$

Problem 1.16 Find 3 different factor trees that you could use to factor out 120, and verify all three of them yield the same prime factorization of 120. What is the prime factorization of 120?

Problem 1.17 What is the sum of the prime factors of 91?

Problem 1.18 Use factor trees to find the prime factorization of 448.

Problem 1.19 What is the sum of the distinct prime factors of 315?

Problem 1.20 Fill in the blanks

(a) $18 \times \underline{\hspace{1cm}} = 14 \times 9$

(b) $42 \times 25 = 21 \times \underline{\hspace{1cm}}$

(c) _____ $\times 24 = 34 \times 36$

Problem 1.21 The product of two numbers is 72 and their sum is 18. What is the smaller of the two numbers?

Problem 1.22 What number multiplied by itself is equal to the product of 32 and 162?

Problem 1.23 Is 281 prime?

Problem 1.24 Dorothy and Bob are counting numbers. Dorothy is counting every three numbers, starting from 3. Bob is counting every five numbers, starting from 5. How many numbers smaller than 50 will both of them count?

Problem 1.25 List all pairs of numbers whose product equals 256. How many such pairs are there?

Problem 1.26 Robert visits his parents every fourth week. His brother Richard visits them every sixth week.

If both Robert and Richard visited their parents last week, how often will both of them visit their parents on the same week?

Problem 1.27 The number 13 is a prime number that yields another prime number when its digits are reversed. How many two-digit prime numbers like this are there?

Problem 1.28 Mr. Bark is a serious money hoarder obsessed with organizing his money in the best, or "prime," way. He wants to arrange a group of 25 dimes into three piles such that each pile contains a different prime number of dimes. What is the greatest number of dimes possible in any of the three piles?

Problem 1.29 Sandy wants to put 300 tires in storage. She will store them by making stacks of tires of the same height.

If she wants the number of stacks of tires to be a multiple of 5, in how many different ways can she store her tires?

Problem 1.30 Consider the numbers 15, 18 and 82.

(a) What is the prime factorization of each of the numbers?

(b) How many factors do each of the numbers have?

(c) What do these numbers have in common?

Problem 1.31 Consider the numbers 16, 100 and 121.

(a) What is the prime factorization of each of the numbers?

(b) How many factors do each of the numbers have?

(c) What do these numbers have in common?

Problem 1.32 Roger has a lock with a keypad. To unlock his lock, Roger must input the two distinct two-digit numbers that are multiples of 18 and 12. He must input the smaller number first, then the second. What sequence of numbers would unlock Roger's lock?

Problem 1.33 What is the smallest possible value of a number that has 6, 14, and 15 as factors?

Problem 1.34 Marisol has tons of sticks of length 10, 12, and 25 inches. She is gluing together sticks of the same size to make larger sticks.

What is the smallest length of one of this larger sticks that she could make with any of the three lengths she has available?

Problem 1.35 Find the smallest number that is a multiple of 5, 21, and 35.

2. Divisibility Rules!

Ricky thinks dividing numbers is fun. He is always excited about finding if numbers are divisible by other numbers. He is always telling people that "Divisibility Rules!".

One of Ricky's favorite car games is looking at the numbers of houses in the street and figuring out fast if the number is divisible by 3. On his most recent trip he saw houses with the numbers 137, 402, 396, 596, and 65536. Which of those are divisible by 3?

The concepts introduced in this chapter directly correspond to Common Core Math Standards as shown in the following table.

3rd Grade	3.OA.9
4th Grade	4.OA.3, 4.OA.4, 4.NBT.2

In addition to the standards above, problems and concepts in this section will help strengthen understanding of the following domains.

3rd Grade	3.OA
4th Grade	4.OA, 4.NBT
5th Grade	5.NBT, 5.NF

2.1 Example Questions

Example 2.1

Oswald needs to pack 945 matches in boxes of 25 matches.
How many boxes does he need?
How many matches will he have left?

Solution

It is not difficult to see that 945 is not a multiple of 25, since all multiples of 25 end in 00, 25, 50, or 75.

The number of boxes he will need will be given by the closest multiple of 25 that does not go over 945. $25 \times 20 = 500$, and $25 \times 40 = 1000$, so the number of boxes will be a little less than 40. Let's take a look.

Boxes	Product	Matches used
40	40×25	1000
39	39×25	975
38	39×25	950
37	37×25	925

We can see that if he uses 37 boxes he can pack 925 matches and will have $945 - 925 = 20$ matches left over.

Quotient, Remainder

In the previous problem we found that 37×25 was the greatest multiple of 25 that was not over 945, and this multiple is 20 less than 945. That is, $945 \div 25 = 37$ with remainder 20.

We call 945 the *dividend*, 25 the *divisor*, 37 the *quotient*, and 20 the *remainder*.

$$\begin{array}{r} 37 \quad \longleftarrow \text{Quotient} \\ \text{Divisor} \longrightarrow 25 \overline{\smash{\big)}\ 945} \quad \longleftarrow \text{Dividend} \\ 20 \quad \longleftarrow \text{Remainder} \end{array}$$

Note we can write $945 = 25 \times 37 + 20$.

Remark

The remainder of a division is always a non-negative integer smaller than the divisor.

If a number a leaves remainder 0 when divided by b, then a is a *multiple* of b.

Example 2.2

Let's help Ricky find which of the house numbers 137, 402, 396, 596, and 65536 are divisible by 3.

Solution

One approach to help out Ricky is to divide the numbers by 3 and see if the remainder is

---

0.

Number	Quotient	Remainder
137	45	2
402	134	0
396	132	0
596	198	2
65536	21845	1

Of course Ricky, with all his experience dividing numbers, knows a few tricks to avoid doing so much work. Instead of dividing each of the number by 3, Ricky adds up the digits of the number and checks if that sum is divisible by 3.

Number	Sum of digits
137	11
402	6
396	18
65536	25

Since 6 and 18 are the only multiples of 3 after adding the digits of the numbers, we can see the only numbers divisible by 3 are 402 and 396 (which we already knew by looking at their quotients and remainders, but this seems like a quicker way to decide).

Note in the case of 396 it wasn't really necessary to add up the digits, since each of the digits is already a multiple of 3, and so their sum would also be a multiple of 3.

Remark

> When the sum of the digits of a number is a number with more than one digit, we can add the digits again until we get a one-digit number.

Divisibility by 3

The remainder of a number when dividing by 3 is the same as the remainder of the sum of its digits. So, a number is divisible by 3 if the sum of its digits is divisible by 3.

Example 2.3

Ricky likes even numbers, and knows that a number is even if the last digit is an even digit. Is there a similar way to decide if a number is divisible by 4, or 8? Help Ricky decide which of 291, 436, 9624, and 68792 are divisible by 4 or 8.

Solution

Let's look at the quotients and remainders when dividing the numbers by 4.

Number	Quotient	Remainder
291	72	3
436	109	0
9624	2406	0
68792	17198	0

From here we can see only 436, 9628, and 68792 are multiples of 4. Looking at their last two digits we can also see they end in a two-digit number that is a multiple of 4 ($36 = 4 \times 9$, $24 = 4 \times 6$, and $92 = 4 \times 23$).

Now let's look at the quotients and remainders when dividing by 8.

Number	Quotient	Remainder
291	36	3
436	54	4
9624	1203	0
68792	8599	0

Since $8 = 4 \times 2$, the only numbers that have a chance of being multiples of 8 are the numbers that were multiples of 4. By looking at the remainders we see only 9624 and 792 are multiples of 8. Look at their *last three digits*, they are all three-digit numbers that are divisible by 8 ($624 = 8 \times 78$, and $792 = 8 \times 99$).

Divisibility by 2, 4, 8

From this example we can conclude that a number
- is divisible by 2 if it ends in a digit that is a multiple of 2
- is divisible by 4 if it ends in a two-digit number that is divisible by 4, and
- is divisible by 8 if it ends in a three-digit number that is divisible by 8

Remark

While we still have to check if the last few digits are divisible by 2, 4, 8, we do not need to divide the whole number to decide if they are divisible. Note, however, that checking if the last few digits are divisible (by 2, 4, or 8) does not give us the quotient.

Example 2.4

Danny has several bags of candy that he wants to share with his 4 friends. He will only share candies from a bag that allows him to give each of his friends and himself the same amount of candy with no leftovers. Which of the following will he share with his friends?
- A bag of candy worms containing 125 worms.
- A bag of gummy bears containing 72 gummy bears.
- A bag of sweet and sour gummies containing 75 gummies.

Solution

Since Danny wants to split his candy among himself and his 4 friends, he needs to check which of the numbers 125, 72, and 75 are divisible by 5.

We can rewrite each of the numbers like $125 = 12 \times 10 + 5$, $72 = 7 \times 10 + 2$, and $75 = 7 \times 10 + 5$. Since $10 = 2 \times 5$, each of these numbers will be a multiple of 5 if the second portion of the sums we wrote is a multiple of 5, that is, if the last digit of the numbers is a multiple of 5. The only single digit numbers that are multiples of 5 are 0 and 5, so a number is a multiple of 5 if it ends in 0 or 5.

Using this rule, we can see almost immediately that 125 and 75 are multiples of 5 (in fact, $125 = 5 \times 25$ and $75 = 5 \times 15$), and 72 is not a multiple of 5.

So Dan will share the candy worms and the sweet and sour gummies with his friends.

Divisibility by 5

A number is divisible by 5 if its last digit is 0 or 5.

Example 2.5

At Mr. Bre D.'s bakery they are having a sale, where a customer gets a 10% discount if they buy a number of pastries that is divisible by 11. There are four customers in line to pay with 132, 150, 778, 924, and 1089 pastries in their carts. Which of them will get the 10% discount?

Solution

The cashier at Mr. Bre D.'s bakery knows a trick to easily find the remainder of a number when dividing by 11. He says that a number is divisible by 11 if the alternating sum of its digits (starting from the last digit) is divisible by 11.

For example, the alternating sum of the digits of 132 is $2 - 3 + 1 = 0$, and 0 is divisible by 11, so 132 is divisible by 11. Let's take a look at the alternating sums of the other numbers as well.

Number	Alternating sum of digits	
132	$2 - 3 + 1$	0
150	$0 - 5 + 1$	-4
778	$8 - 7 + 7$	8
924	$4 - 2 + 9$	11
1089	$9 - 8 + 0 - 1$	0

According to the cashier's trick, looking at the alternating sums of the digits of numbers, we can see 132, 924 and 1089 are multiples of 11, and 150 and 778 are not multiples of 11. So only the customers with 132, 924, and 1089 pastries will get the discount.

Alternating sum of digits

We can find the alternating sum of the digits of a number by alternating adding and subtracting the digits of the number, starting from the right most digit. For example, the alternating sum of the digits of 452 is $2 - 5 + 4 = 1$, and the alternating sum of the digits of 2019 is $9 - 1 + 0 - 2 = 6$.

Divisibility by 11

A number is divisible by 11 if the alternating sum of its digits is divisible by 11.

Remark

Note the alternating sum of the digits of a number gives us more than just a way to decide if the numbers are divisible by 11. We can see 150 is 4 less than a multiple of 11, and so it is $11 - 4 = 7$ more than a multiple of 11 ($150 = 11 \times 13 + 7$); and 778 is 8 more than a multiple of 11 ($778 = 11 \times 70 + 8$).

Example 2.6

Which of the numbers 658, 630, 975, and 940 are
  (a) divisible by 6?
  (b) divisible by 10?

Solution to Part (a)

$6 = 2 \times 3$, and 2 and 3 are distinct prime numbers, so a number is divisible by 6 if it is divisible by 2 and by 3.

So, a number is divisible by 6 if (i) it ends in 0, 2, 4, 6, or 8, and (ii) the sum of its digits is divisible by 3.

Let's take a look at the last digit of the numbers and to the sum of their digits.

Number	Last Digit	Sum of digits
658	8	17
630	0	9
975	5	21
940	0	13

We can see that the numbers that are multiples of 2 are 658, 630, and 940, and the numbers that are divisible by 3 are 630, and 975. So the only number that is divisible by 6 is 630 (in fact, $630 = 6 \times 105$).

Solution to Part (b)

$10 = 2 \times 5$, and 2 and 5 are distinct prime numbers, so a number is divisible by 10 if it is divisible by 2 and 5.

A number is divisible by 2 if it ends in an even digit, and is divisible by 5 if it ends in 5 or 0. So, a number is divisible by 10 if it ends in 0.

From the list, the numbers that end in 0 are 630 and 940, so they are divisible by 10.

Example 2.7

Ricky recently learned that he can check if a number is divisible by 9 in the same way he can check if a number is divisible by 3.
Help Ricky decide which of 657, 6997, 2340, and 34596 are divisible by 9.

Solution

Let's take a look at the sum of the digits of each of the numbers.

Number	Sum of digits
657	18
6997	31
2340	9
34596	27

18, 9, and 27 are all multiples of 9, while 31 is not. This means 657, 2340, and 34596 are multiples of 9 (in fact, $657 = 9 \times 73$, $2340 = 9 \times 260$, and $34596 = 9 \times 3844$), and 6997 is not a multiple of 9 ($6997 = 777 \times 9 + 4$).

Divisibility by 9

A number is divisible by 9 if the sum of its digits is divisible by 9.

Divisibility Rules

We can summarize all the divisibility rules we've learned so far:

Number	Rule
2	The number ends in 0, 2, 4, 6, or 8.
3	The sum of the digits of the number divisible by 3.
4	The number formed by the last two digits of the number is divisible by 4.
5	The number ends in 0 or 5.
6	The number is divisible by 2 and by 3.
8	The number formed by the last three digits of the number is divisible by 4.
9	The sum of the digits of the number is divisible by 9.
10	The number ends in 0.
11	The alternating sum of the digits of the number is divisible by 11.

Example 2.8

Which of 132, 180 and 990 are
  (a) divisible by 22?
  (b) divisible by 36
  (c) divisible by 45

Solution to Part (a)

$22 = 2 \times 11$. 2 and 11 are distinct primes, so a number is a multiple of 22 if it is a multiple of 2 and 11.

All numbers in the list are even, so we just need to check which are divisible by 11.

- The alternating sum of the digits of 132 is $2 - 3 + 1 = 0$, so it is divisible by 11.
- The alternating sum of the digits of 180 is $0 - 8 + 1 = -7$, so 180 is not divisible by 11.
- The alternating sum of the digits of 990 is $0 - 9 + 9 = 0$, so it is divisible by 11.

Thus, only 132 and 990 are multiples of 22.

Solution to Part (b)

$36 = 2 \times 2 \times 3 \times 3$. 2 and 3 are distinct prime numbers, so a number is divisible by 36 if it is divisible by $2 \times 2 = 4$ and divisible by $3 \times 3 = 9$. (Note is is not enough to check that the number is divisible by 2 and 3, since there are numbers that are divisible by 6 that are not divisible by 36, for example, 42.)

Number	Last two digits	Sum of digits
132	32	6
180	80	9
990	90	18

So 132 and 180 are divisible by 4, and 180 and 990 are divisible by 9. Thus, only 180 is divisible by 36.

Solution to Part (c)

$45 = 3 \times 3 \times 5$. 3 and 5 are distinct prime numbers, so a number is divisible by 45 if it is divisible by $3 \times 3 = 9$ and by 5. (Again, it is not enough to check if the number is divisible by just 3, since 3 appears twice in the prime factorization of 45.)

On part (b) we found that 180 and 990 are divisible by 9, and since both end in 0, they are also divisible by 5. Thus 180 and 990 are divisible by 45.

Example 2.9

Leeann is passionate about making and selling candles. She recently made 72 blue scented candles, and 60 purple scented candles.
She wants to make sure to pack them all in boxes of equal size, so that each box has candles of one kind only (so all blue or all purple).

How many candles should she pack in each box to make sure she has no candles left over? How many boxes would she need?

What is the largest number of candles she could pack in each box?

Solution

The number of candles in each box must be a number that divides 72, the number of blue scented candles, and also 60, the number of purple scented candles.

We can use factor trees to find the prime factorization of 72 and 60:

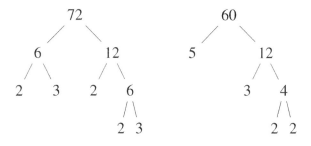

So
$$72 = 2 \times 2 \times 2 \times 2 \times 3 \times 3$$

and
$$60 = 2 \times 2 \times 3 \times 5.$$

Now we can find all factors of 72 and all factors of 60:

72		60	
Primes	Factor	Primes	Factor
	1		1
2	2	2	2
2×2	4	2×2	4
$2 \times 2 \times 2$	8	3	3
3	3	2×3	6
2×3	6	$2 \times 2 \times 3$	12
$2 \times 2 \times 3$	12	5	5
$2 \times 2 \times 2 \times 3$	24	2×5	10
3×3	9	$2 \times 2 \times 5$	20
$2 \times 3 \times 3$	18	3×5	15
$2 \times 2 \times 3 \times 3$	36	$2 \times 3 \times 5$	30
$2 \times 2 \times 2 \times 3 \times 3$	72	$2 \times 2 \times 3 \times 5$	60

Here we can see that 1, 2, 3, 4, 6, and 12, are all the *common divisors* of 72 and 60, so Leeann could use any of those as the number of candles to pack in each box.

If she were to choose to pack 2 candles per box, she would need $72 \div 2 = 36$ boxes for the blue candles and $60 \div 2 = 30$ boxes for the purple candles, $36 + 30 = 66$ boxes in total.

We can do something similar to figure out how many boxes she would need in each of the other cases. The possible number of boxes are summarized in the table below.

Candles per box	Boxes needed		
	Blue	Purple	Total
1	72	60	132
2	36	30	66
3	24	20	44
4	18	15	33
6	12	10	22
12	6	5	11

The maximum number of candles per box that Leeann can use is 12. Notice packing 12 candles per box yields the smallest number of boxes needed to pack all the candles.

Common divisor

If a number d divides both a and b, we say d is a *common divisor of a and b*.

Remark

1 is always a divisor of any number, thus any two numbers always have at least one common divisor.

Greatest Common Divisor (GCD)

If d is the largest number that divides both a and b, we say d is the *Greatest Common Divisor* (or *GCD* for short). The GCD of a and b is usually denoted by $\gcd(a,b)$.

Remark

Oftentimes the words divisor and factor are used interchangeably, so the Greatest Common Divisor of two numbers is also referred to as their Greatest Common Factor (or GCF).

Example 2.10

Given her success in packing candles, Leeann decided to do it once more. This time she made 144 red scented candles and 216 green scented candles. What is the largest number of candles she can pack in a box so all boxes have the same number of candles and each box contains only candles of one kind?

Solution 1

To find the largest number of candles Leeann can pack in one box we need to find the largest number that divides both 144 and 216, that is, we need to find the GCD of 144 and 216.

To find the GCD of two numbers, instead of listing all of the factors of each number to find the largest that divides both, we can use a table (similar to the one we used to find the LCM of two numbers) to help us out. Start with the numbers on the top, like so

Then, proceed as we did with the LCM, but this time keep track of the prime numbers that you used to divide numbers in *both columns* at the same time (we'll do it with a ☐

here):

	144	216
2	72	108
2	36	54
2	18	27
2	9	27
3	3	9
3	1	3
3		1

The GCD of the numbers is the product of all the boxed prime numbers on the left, so the GCD of 144 and 216 is $2 \times 2 \times 2 \times 3 \times 3 = 72$.

Solution 2

Alternatively, we can also factor each of the numbers and look at the prime factors that they have in common.

Using factor trees

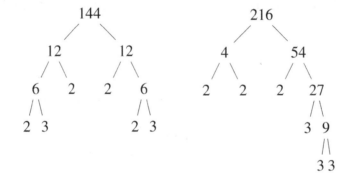

we see that

$$144 = 2 \times 2 \times 2 \times 2 \times 3 \times 3$$

and

$$216 = 2 \times 2 \times 2 \times 3 \times 3 \times 3.$$

List all the prime factors of each of the numbers and put them side by side. Then for each of the different prime factors, look at which has the *least* repetitions, so this is how many times this prime factor will be a factor of the GCD of the two numbers.

In this case, we have

144	$2 \times 2 \times 2 \times 2$	$\times 3 \times 3$	
216	$2 \times 2 \times 2$	$\times 3 \times 3 \times 3$	
GCD	$2 \times 2 \times 2$	$\times 3 \times 3$	$= 72$

Remark

Note with the two methods to find the GCD that we just showed, it is possible to find the LCM *at the same time*.

GCD LCM

$\downarrow$	$\downarrow$	144	216
2	2	72	108
2	2	36	54
2	2	18	27
2	2	9	27
3	3	3	9
3	3	1	3
3	3		1

144	$2 \times 2 \times 2 \times 2$	$\times 3 \times 3$	
216	$2 \times 2 \times 2$	$\times 3 \times 3 \times 3$	
GCD	$2 \times 2 \times 2$	$\times 3 \times 3$	$= 72$
LCM	$2 \times 2 \times 2 \times 2$	$\times 3 \times 3 \times 3$	$= 432$

2.2 Quick Response Questions

Problem 2.1 What is the quotient and remainder when 98 is divided by 5?

(A) Quotient: 17, Remainder: 3
(B) Quotient: 18, Remainder: 8
(C) Quotient: 19, Remainder: 3
(D) Quotient: 19, Remainder: 8

Problem 2.2 What is the sum of the digits of 219?

Problem 2.3 Is 219 divisible by 3? Why?

(A) Yes, because its last digit is divisible by 3.
(B) Yes, because the sum of its digits is divisible by 3.
(C) Yes, because the sum of its digits is 3.
(D) No, because the sum of its digits is not 3.

Problem 2.4 Is 219 divisible by 9?

Problem 2.5 Only one of the numbers 668, 686, and 866 is divisible by 4. Which number is it?

Problem 2.6 What is the alternating sum of the digits of 495?

Problem 2.7 Is 495 divisible by 11? Why?

(A) Yes, because the sum of its digits is divisible by 11.
(B) Yes, because the alternating sum of its digits is divisible by 11.
(C) No, because the sum of its digits is not divisible by 11.
(D) No, because the alternating sum of its digits is not divisible by 11.

Problem 2.8 Is 384 divisible by 2, by 3, and/or by 6?

(A) divisible by 2 only
(B) divisible by 3 only
(C) divisible by 2 and 3 but not 6
(D) divisible by 2, 3, and 6

Problem 2.9 What is the GCD and LCM of the 11 and 25?

(A) GCD: 1, LCM: 275
(B) GCD: 11, LCM: 275
(C) GCD: 275, LCM: 1
(D) GCD: 1, LCM: 550

Problem 2.10 What is the GCD and LCM of the 15 and 45?

(A) GCD: 5, LCM: 90
(B) GCD: 3, LCM: 225
(C) GCD: 15, LCM: 45
(D) GCD: 15, LCM: 90

2.3 Practice

Problem 2.11 Which of the following are divisible by 3?

(a) 2352

(b) 3701

(c) 4013

Problem 2.12 Which of the numbers

$$234, 243, 324, 342, 423, \text{ and } 432$$

are divisible by 4?

Problem 2.13 Which of the following are divisible by 5?

(a) 543

(b) 685

(c) 935

Problem 2.14 Which of the following are divisible by 6?

(a) 476

(b) 162

(c) 282

Problem 2.15 Which of the following are divisible by 8?

(a) 1158

(b) 1184

(c) 1258

Problem 2.16 Which of the numbers

$$2376, 2367, 7632, 3276, 6723, \text{ and } 7326$$

are divisible by 9?

Problem 2.17 Which of the following are divisible by 11?

(a) 924

(b) 111

(c) 295

Problem 2.18 Which of 660, 825, and 924 are

(a) divisible by 28?

(b) divisible by 66?

(c) divisible by 75?

Problem 2.19 What are the LCM and GCD of:

(a) 215 and 645

(b) 242 and 605

(c) 180 and 180

Problem 2.20 Megan has to put away 985 colored pencils into boxes of 25 pencils. How many boxes does she need? How many pencils will she have left?

Problem 2.21 Donny is at the beach. He counts 16 seagulls, 19 sand crabs, and 22 beach umbrellas. Which of these could be grouped in pairs with no leftovers?

Problem 2.22 Bobby is at the store and wants to buy one new tooth brush. Bobby is choosing among a premium tooth brush that costs $16, a tooth brush for sensitive teeth that costs $22, and a tooth brush/travel toothbrush combo for $23.

Bobby has only $2 bills and the cashier at the store has no change. Which of these tooth brushes could Bobby buy?

Problem 2.23 Joseph had 431 stamps. He put them into 4 different stamp books, with the same number of stamps in each stamp book.

If Joseph used as many stamps as he could, how many stamps were in each stamp book? How many stamps did he have left over?

Problem 2.24 Brian wrote the numbers 261, 332, 118, and 302 in small pieces of paper and put them inside a hat. He then asked his friends to draw one at random. The winner would be whoever draws a number that is a multiple of 4.

Which of these numbers would be the winning number?

Problem 2.25 Conner has 525 beads. He wants to place them into boxes containing the same number of beads each, with no beads left over. If he wants to use at least 2 boxes and no more than 20 boxes, how many boxes could he use? How many beads would he place per box in each case?

Problem 2.26 Leah bought some rings at the mall. She paid the same amount for each one, and her total was $165. If she paid somewhere between $20 and $35 per ring, how many rings did she buy?

Problem 2.27 Diana is the assistant to the principal at school. The students of 5th and 6th grade soon will go on a school trip so she is making check-in lists with the names of all students. She is arranging them in pages that have 4 columns of 18 students each.

If there are 210 students on the 5th grade and 355 students on the 6th grade, how many pages will she need for each grade?

Problem 2.28 Barry made 78 sandwiches, using 6 different meats. If he made the same number of each type of sandwich, how many sandwiches of each kind did he make?

Problem 2.29 Mr. Harper is getting boxes of snacks for the students at his school. He wants to give the same number of snacks to each of the eight 6th grade classes. At the store they have boxes with 2140, 3240, and 4340 snacks.

If Mr. Harper plans on buying only one box, which box would allow him to give the same number of snacks to each class with no left overs?

Problem 2.30 There are 72 boys and 90 girls in the school patio. Mr. Bonfire wants to divide them into groups, where each group has the same number of boys and the same number of girls.

If Mr. Bonfire wants to have as many teams as possible, how many girls will there be in each team?

Problem 2.31 Andy and Dany work at a warehouse packing bottles of soda.

Andy packs his bottles in groups of 9, and Dany packs his bottles in groups of 12.

Which of the following shipments could have been prepared by Andy or Dany?

(a) A shipment with 270 bottles.

(b) A shipment with 648 bottles.

(c) A shipment with 520 bottles.

Problem 2.32 Andrew works at a local amusement park keeping track of the number of guests entering the park during his shift. Just for fun, at the end of his shift he checks if the number of tickets he received is divisible by 11.

Over the past five days he's counted 3223, 3280, 2695, 3308, and 4630 guests. Which of those are multiples of 11?

Problem 2.33 There are 56 fifth graders and 70 sixth graders in the gym. Coach Rogers wants to arrange them in equal rows with only fifth graders or only sixth graders in each row. What is the greatest number of students that can be in each row?

Problem 2.34 Jake likes palindromes (numbers that can be read the same left to right than right to left) and multiples of 11. Help Jake find examples of the following:

(a) A palindrome with an even number of digits that is a multiple of 11.

(b) A palindrome with an odd number of digits that is a multiple of 11.

(c) A palindrome that is not a multiple of 11.

Problem 2.35 Brad has 120 red toy cars, 280 green toy cars, and 100 blue toy cars. He wants to arrange them in rows with only cars of the same color per row. If he wants to have all rows the same size and as big as possible, how many rows of green cars would he have?

3. Pizza Slices

Sally and Mae went to their favorite pizza place for dinner. Sally ordered a large pizza with 6 equal sized slices. Mae also ordered a large pizza, but hers came with 12 equal sized slices.

At first, Sally ate 2 slices of pizza and Mae ate 3 slices of pizza. Who ate the most pizza?

The concepts introduced in this chapter directly correspond to Common Core Math Standards as shown in the following table.

3rd Grade	3.NF.1, 3.NF.3
4th Grade	4.NF.1, 4.NF.2, 4.NF.3, 4.NF.4
5th Grade	5.NF.1, 5.NF.2, 5.NF.3, 5.NF.4, 5.NF.6, 5.NF.7

In addition to the standards above, problems and concepts in this section will help strengthen understanding of the following domains.

3rd Grade	3.OA, 3.NBT, 3.NF
4th Grade	4.OA, 4.NBT, 4.NF
5th Grade	5.NBT, 5.NF

3.1 Example Questions

Example 3.1

Stella and 3 of her friends decided to get some pizza. They ordered 3 small pizzas, each with 8 slices, and decided to split them evenly among the 4 of them.

How much pizza will each of them eat?

Solution

There are $3 \times 8 = 24$ slices for them to share. Since they want to divide evenly the number of slices they get, each of them would get $24 \div 4 = 6$ slices of pizza.

One whole pizza comes with 8 slices, and each is eating 6 of them. If we want to represent this portion of a whole pizza with a number we can use fractions, which are used to represent parts of a whole. To write a fraction we use two numbers: a number called denominator that tells us in how many equal parts we have divided our whole, and a number called numerator that tells us how many of those equal parts the fraction represents.

For example, to represent the portion of pizza that Stella and her friends ate, we can use the fraction

$$\frac{6 \quad \longleftarrow \quad \text{numerator}}{8 \quad \longleftarrow \quad \text{denominator}}$$

since each of them is eating 6 slices out of the 8 that come in a pizza. So, we can say each of them ate $\dfrac{6}{8}$ of a pizza.

Fraction

Fractions represent portions of a whole. For example, the following shaded portion

is represented by the fraction

$$\dfrac{5}{8} \begin{array}{l} \longleftarrow \text{ numerator} \\ \longleftarrow \text{ denominator} \end{array}$$

The denominator of a fraction tells us in how many equal sized pieces we split the whole, and the numerator tells us how many of those pieces the fraction represents.

Example 3.2

Karla has a bar of chocolate that she wants to enjoy throughout the day. She splits her bar of chocolate in 12 equal pieces and eats 3 pieces right away. Later that day she ate 2 more pieces of her chocolate, and saved the rest to eat after dinner.

(a) How much of her chocolate has she eaten so far?
(b) How much of her chocolate does she have left to eat after dinner?

Solution to Part (a)

Since she split her chocolate in 12 equal sized pieces, each of the pieces of her chocolate represents $\dfrac{1}{12}$ of her chocolate.

First she eats 3 pieces and then she eats 2 more pieces, so she eats $3 + 2 = 5$ of the 12 pieces of chocolate

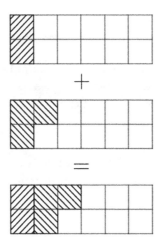

Since each piece represents $\dfrac{1}{12}$ of her chocolate, this represents $\dfrac{5}{12}$ of the chocolate.

Note the numerator of our resulting fraction is equal to the sum of the numerators of the fractions we are adding, and the denominator stayed the same, that is,

$$\frac{2}{12} + \frac{3}{12} = \frac{2+3}{12} = \frac{5}{12}$$

Solution to Part (b)

The fraction $\dfrac{12}{12}$ represents the whole chocolate, since we are taking all 12 pieces. From these, we want to take away the 5 pieces she's eaten already, so she will be left with $12 - 5 = 7$ pieces of chocolate.

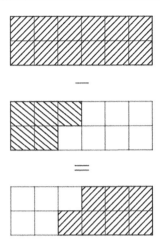

This time the numerator of the resulting fraction is equal to the difference of the numerators of the fractions we subtracted, and, once again, the denominator stayed the same, that is,

$$\frac{12}{12} - \frac{5}{12} = \frac{12-5}{12} = \frac{7}{12},$$

so Karla still has $\dfrac{7}{12}$ of her chocolate left to eat after dinner.

Fractions with like denominators

Fractions that have the same denominator referred to as fractions with *like denominators*.

Add & subtract fractions with like denominators

To add/subtract fractions with like denominators we add/subtract the numerators and keep the same denominator. For example

$$\frac{2}{12} + \frac{3}{12} = \frac{2+3}{12} = \frac{5}{12}$$

and

$$\frac{12}{12} - \frac{5}{12} = \frac{12-5}{12} = \frac{7}{12}.$$

Example 3.3

Sally and Mae went to their favorite pizza place for dinner. Sally ordered a large pizza with 6 equal sized slices. Mae also ordered a large pizza, but hers came with 12 equal sized slices.

(a) At first, Sally ate 2 slices of pizza and Mae ate 3 slices of pizza. Who ate the most pizza?

(b) After eating some more pizza, they decided to take the leftovers home. As it turns out, both of them took home $\frac{1}{3}$ of their pizzas. How many slices of pizza did each of them take home?

Solution to Part (a)

Sally ate 2 of her 6 slices, so she ate $\frac{2}{6}$ of her pizza. Mae ate 3 of her 12 slices, so she ate $\frac{3}{12}$ of her pizza.

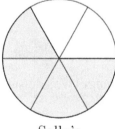   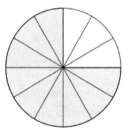

Sally's   Mae's

From the diagrams, it is not difficult to see that Sally ate the most pizza. To decide who ate the most pizza without looking at the diagram, we need to see which of the fractions $\frac{2}{6}$ and $\frac{3}{12}$ represents a bigger portion of the pizza.

Since Mae's pizza was cut in 12 slices and Sally's was cut in 6 slices, Mae's slices are twice as big. That is, 1 slice of Sally's pizza has the same size as 2 of Mae's slices. Thus, since Sally ate 2 of her 6 slices, that is as if she had eaten $2 \times 2 = 4$ slices of a pizza sliced in $6 \times 2 = 12$ slices.

So, Sally ate $\frac{4}{12}$ of her pizza and Mae ate $\frac{3}{12}$ of her pizza. Now that we have fractions with the same denominator, we can compare them by looking at their numerators. Sally's fraction has a bigger numerator, so she ate the most pizza.

Solution to Part (b)

To see how many slices they took home, we need to find fractions with denominator 6 and 12 that represent the same portion as $\frac{1}{3}$ does.

Let's start with a pizza sliced in 3 big slices. If we split each of this slices in 2 equal slices, we would have a total of $3 \times 2 = 6$ slices, as in Sally's pizza.

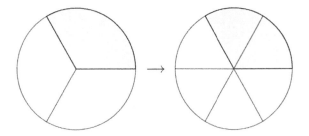

So, 1 slice that is $\frac{1}{3}$ of a pizza is the same as 2 slices that are $\frac{1}{6}$, that is,

$$\frac{1}{3} = \frac{1 \times 2}{3 \times 2} = \frac{2}{6}.$$

If we start once again with a pizza sliced in 3, we can split each of the slices in 4, to obtain a total of $3 \times 4 = 12$ slices, as in Mae's pizza.

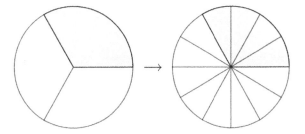

So 1 slice that is $\frac{1}{3}$ of a pizza is the same as 4 slices that are $\frac{1}{12}$, that is,

$$\frac{1}{3} = \frac{1 \times 4}{3 \times 4} = \frac{4}{12}.$$

Therefore, Sally took home 2 slices of pizza and Mae took home 4 slices of pizza.

Remark

It is always possible to represent the same part of a whole by using different fractions.

Equivalent Fraction

If two fractions that have different numerator and denominator represent the same part of a whole, we say the two fractions are *equivalent*.

For example, $\frac{1}{3}$, $\frac{2}{6}$, and $\frac{4}{12}$ are equivalent fractions.

Remark

Given a fraction we can find other fractions that are equivalent to it by multiplying or dividing the numerator *and* the denominator by the *same number*.

Example 3.4

Sophie is learning about fractions in school and she is working on her homework assignment. She knows there is not a unique fraction that she can give as an answer, and she'd rather use fractions that have numbers that are as small as possible before she turns in her homework assignment.

For each of Sophie's fractions below, help her find an equivalent fraction that uses numbers that are as small as possible.

(a) $\dfrac{12}{20}$

(b) $\dfrac{16}{72}$

(c) $\dfrac{5}{14}$

Solution to Part (a)

We know that, given a fraction, we can find other fractions that are equivalent to it by multiplying or dividing by the same number on both the numerator and the denominator of the fraction.

Sophie's goal is to find a fraction that is equivalent to $\dfrac{12}{20}$ that uses numbers that are as small as possible. Multiplying the numerator and denominator of her fraction would yield numbers that are bigger, so that's definitely not the way to go.

Both 12 and 20 are even numbers, so we can divide both by 2. This yields the fraction

$$\frac{12}{20} = \frac{12 \div 2}{20 \div 2} = \frac{6}{10}.$$

This new fraction has numbers that are still divisible by 2, so we can divide both by 2 once more:

$$\frac{6}{10} = \frac{6 \div 2}{10 \div 2} = \frac{3}{5}.$$

Now the numerator and the denominator of the fraction do not have any common divisors (other than 1), so we won't be able to divide any further to find smaller numbers. This means the simplest way to write the fraction $\dfrac{12}{20}$ is $\dfrac{3}{5}$.

Solution to Part (b)

On the previous example we found that, in order to find an equivalent fraction with numbers that are as small as possible, we must divide both the numerator and the denominator of $\dfrac{16}{72}$ by the same number, and this number should be as large as possible. That is, we need to divide both 16 and 72 by their largest common divisor, that is, the GCD of 16 and 72.

Since $16 = 2 \times 2 \times 2 \times 2$ and $72 = 2 \times 2 \times 2 \times 3 \times 3$, the GCD of 16 and 72 is $2 \times 2 \times 2 = 8$. Dividing the numerator and denominator by 8 we obtain

$$\frac{16}{72} = \frac{16 \div 8}{72 \div 8} = \frac{2}{9}.$$

Observe this new fraction cannot be simplified any further, since the only common divisor of 2 and 9 is 1. This makes sense, since we already divided the numerator and denominator by the largest number we could find.

In general, the best way to find the simplest version of a fraction (so, an equivalent fraction with the numerator and denominator as small as possible), is to use the GCD of the numerator and denominator. This is probably one of the most useful applications of the GCD of two numbers.

Solution to Part (c)

The GCD of 5 and 14 is 1, since 5 is a prime number and 14 is not divisible by 5. Thus, the fraction $\dfrac{5}{14}$ is already simplified as much as possible.

Fraction in lowest terms

If the GCD of the numerator and the denominator of a fraction is 1, we say the fraction is a *simplified fraction* or a *fraction in lowest terms*.

Whenever the numerator and the denominator of a fraction have a GCD that is not 1, we can find the simplest version of this fraction by dividing both the numerator and the denominator by their GCD.

> ### Example 3.5
>
> Danny has a long homework assignment from his French class. When he came home from school he was able to complete $\dfrac{3}{10}$ of his assignment before dinner. He then completed $\dfrac{7}{15}$ of his assignment after dinner.
>
> What fraction of his homework assignment has he completed so far?

Solution

To figure out what fraction of his assignment he has completed so far, we need to add the fractions $\dfrac{3}{10}$ and $\dfrac{7}{15}$. This fractions have different denominators, so we cannot just add the numerators as we did on a previous problem.

Since we already know how to add fractions with like denominators, the first thing we will do is find fractions that are equivalent to $\dfrac{3}{10}$ and $\dfrac{7}{15}$ that have the same denominator (we call this denominator the common denominator).

Any common multiple of 10 and 15 will work as our common denominator. To work with numbers that are as small as possible it is good practice to use the LCM of the two denominators as a common denominator.

The LCM of 10 and 15 is 30, and $30 = 10 \times 3$ so, if we multiply both the numerator and the denominator of $\dfrac{3}{10}$ by 3, we will obtain an equivalent fraction with denominator 30:

$$\frac{3}{10} = \frac{3 \times 3}{10 \times 3} = \frac{9}{30}.$$

Similarly, as $30 = 15 \times 2$, if we multiply both the numerator and the denominator of $\dfrac{7}{15}$ by 2, we will obtain an equivalent fraction with denominator 30:

$$\frac{7}{15} = \frac{7 \times 2}{15 \times 2} = \frac{14}{30}.$$

Now that we have found equivalent fractions with the same denominator, we can add the fractions:

$$\frac{3}{10} + \frac{7}{15} = \frac{9}{30} + \frac{14}{30} = \frac{9+14}{30} = \frac{23}{30},$$

so Danny has completed $\dfrac{23}{30}$ of his assignment.

Add & subtract fractions with different denominators

To add/subtract fractions with different denominators, start by finding equivalent fractions that have the same denominator. This denominator is often referred to as the *common denominator*.

The smallest common denominator that can be used is the LCM of the denominators of the fractions. Once both fractions have the same denominator, proceed to add/subtract them by adding/subtracting their numerators.

Example 3.6

For her birthday party, Carmen baked 40 cupcakes. Some of her friends helped her set up for the party, and while they were at it, they ate $\dfrac{1}{5}$ of the cupcakes. Later, within the first hour of the party, $\dfrac{3}{4}$ of the remaining cupcakes were gone.
  (a) What fraction of the cupcakes were eaten during the first hour of the party?
  (b) How many cupcakes cupcakes is that?

Solution to Part (a)

Arrange the cupcakes in a 4×5 grid. Since $4 \times 5 = 20$ and there are 40 cupcakes, there should be $40 \div 20 = 2$ cupcakes in each rectangle in the grid, as in the diagram below.

The 5 columns of the grid help us visualize the fractions with denominator 5, and the 4 rows help us visualize the fractions with denominator 4.

At first Carmen's friends ate $\dfrac{1}{5}$ of the cupcakes, so we can get rid of one of the 5 columns

and we are left with only $\dfrac{5}{5} - \dfrac{1}{5} = \dfrac{4}{5}$ of the cupcakes.

From these, the guests of the party ate $\dfrac{3}{4}$ of the cupcakes, so we can think they ate the remaining cupcakes in the first three rows of the grid.

Observe the cupcakes that the guests ate during the first hour of the party occupy $3 \times 4 = 12$ of the rectangles in the grid. There are 20 rectangles in total, so this represents $\dfrac{12}{20}$ of the cupcakes.

Since we found $\dfrac{12}{20}$ is $\dfrac{3}{4}$ of $\dfrac{4}{5}$, what we actually did was

$$\frac{3}{4} \times \frac{4}{5} = \frac{12}{20}.$$

Note we obtained the numerator of 12 by multiplying the numerators 3 and 4, and we obtained the denominator of 20 by multiplying the denominators 4 and 5.

The GCD of 12 and 20 is 4, so we can simplify our fraction by dividing the numerator and denominator by 4

$$\frac{12}{20} = \frac{12 \div 4}{20 \div 4} = \frac{3}{5}.$$

Thus, $\dfrac{3}{5}$ of the cupcakes were eaten during the first hour of the party.

Solution to Part (b)

From the grid, we can see this fraction represents $12 \times 2 = 24$ cupcakes. We can also figure this out without looking at the grid.

We want to know how many cupcakes are equal to $\dfrac{3}{5}$ of 40 cupcakes, so we want to do

$$\frac{3}{5} \times 40.$$

We can always regard an integer as a fraction by using 1 as denominator, so we have

$$\frac{3}{5} \times \frac{40}{1} = \frac{3 \times 40}{5 \times 1} = 3 \times 40 \div 5 = 3 \times 8 = 24$$

cupcakes.

Multiplication of Fractions

In general, to multiply fractions, we multiply the numerators together to obtain the numerator of the product, and we multiply the denominators together to obtain the denominator of the product:

$$\frac{a}{b} \times \frac{c}{d} = \frac{a \times c}{b \times d}.$$

Remark

It is always possible to rewrite an integer so it looks like a fraction by keeping the integer in the numerator and using denominator 1, that is,

$$n = \frac{n}{1}.$$

This proves useful when doing arithmetic operations that involve fractions and integers.

Example 3.7

Justin just learned how to multiply fractions and has been practicing his skills. One particular exercise that got his attention asked him to find the product of $\frac{5}{14}$ and $\frac{14}{5}$. What is this product equal to?

Solution

To multiply the fractions we multiply the numerators and the denominators

$$\frac{5}{14} \times \frac{14}{5} = \frac{5 \times 14}{14 \times 5} = \frac{70}{70} = 1.$$

So, the product of these fractions is equal to 1. Note one of the fractions can be obtained by flipping over the numerator and the denominator of the other. We call $\frac{14}{5}$ the reciprocal of $\frac{5}{14}$.

When multiplying a fraction by its reciprocal, the product is always equal to 1, as we obtain the same product in the numerator and the denominator. Since

$$\frac{5}{14} \times \frac{14}{5} = 1,$$

we can also say that

$$1 \div \frac{5}{14} = \frac{14}{5}.$$

Reciprocal of a Fraction

The fraction obtained by flipping over the numerator and the denominator of a fraction is called its *reciprocal*.

Example 3.8

Anthony is preparing some materials for his crafts class. He's got 2 ribbons, each
of length 20 inches, and needs to cut them into smaller ribbons.
  (a) How many pieces of ribbon will he get if he cuts one of the ribbons in equal
       pieces that are 4 inches long?
  (b) How many pieces of ribbon will he get if he cuts the other ribbon in equal
       pieces that are $\frac{5}{7}$ of an inch long?

Solution to Part (a)

To find how many pieces of ribbon he would obtain, we can divide the length of the
ribbon by the length of the desired smaller ribbons. That is, he would obtain $20 \div 4 = 5$
pieces of ribbon of length 4 inches.

Observe $20 \div 4$ is the same as $\frac{1}{4}$ of 20, that is,

$$20 \div 4 = 20 \times \frac{1}{4} = \frac{20}{1} \times \frac{1}{4} = \frac{20}{4} = 5,$$

so we can say "dividing by 4" is the same as "multiplying by $\frac{1}{4}$".

As a fraction, 4 can be written as $\frac{4}{1}$, and $\frac{1}{4}$ is its reciprocal, so

$$20 \div \frac{4}{1} = 20 \times \frac{1}{4}.$$

In other words, dividing by $\frac{4}{1}$ is the same as multiplying by its reciprocal $\frac{1}{4}$.

Solution to Part (b)

We can proceed similarly to the previous part. To find how many pieces of ribbon we
would obtain, we need to divide the total length of the long ribbon by the length of the
smaller desired pieces of ribbon.

Thus, we want to do $20 \div \frac{5}{7}$. As we observed before, dividing by a fraction is the same as multiplying by its reciprocal. Therefore, Anthony would obtain

$$20 \div \frac{5}{7} = 20 \times \frac{7}{5} = \frac{20 \times 7}{5} = \frac{140}{5} = 28$$

pieces of ribbon that are $\frac{5}{7}$ of an inch long.

When we did $\frac{20 \times 7}{5}$, it is also possible to simplify before multiplying 20×7, so we work with smaller numbers. Since $20 = 4 \times 5$, we have

$$\frac{20 \times 7}{5} = \frac{4 \times 5 \times 7}{5} = \frac{4 \times 7}{1} = 28.$$

Dividing by Fractions

Dividing by a fraction is the same as multiplying by its reciprocal, so

$$\frac{a}{b} \div \frac{c}{d} = \frac{a}{b} \times \frac{d}{c}.$$

Example 3.9

Alexa, Billy, and Candace helped organize a pizza party for their class. They ordered 5 pepperoni pizzas, 3 Hawaiian BBQ pizzas, and 4 cheese pizzas. All pizzas were the same size and had 8 slices each. At the end of the party they counted how many slices of pizza were left. They counted 12 pepperoni pizza slices, 7 Hawaiian BBQ pizza slices, and 11 cheese pizza slices.

How much pizza was left after the party?

Solution

Since all pizzas came with 8 slices, they have

$$\frac{12}{8} + \frac{7}{8} + \frac{11}{8} = \frac{12+7+1}{8} = \frac{20}{8}$$

of a pizza leftover.

In the fraction $\frac{20}{8}$, the numerator is greater than the denominator, so this fraction represents more than 1 whole pizza.

To figure out how many whole pizzas this fraction represents, we can divide the numerator by the denominator. $20 \div 8$ is equal to 2 with remainder 4, so this fraction represents 2 whole pizzas and $\frac{4}{8}$ of a pizza.

A fraction whose numerator is greater than or equal to its denominator is called an improper fraction, since it represents at least one whole. When we find how many "wholes" and what fractional part of a whole this improper fraction represents, we can write a *mixed number* that consists of an integer and a proper fraction (a fraction whose numerator is smaller than the denominator).

$$8\overline{\smash{\big)}20} \quad \longleftrightarrow \quad 2\frac{4}{8} = 2\frac{1}{2}$$

When we divide the numerator by the denominator, the quotient becomes the integer part, and the remainder becomes the numerator of the fractional part, while the denominator stays the same. We can then simplify the fractional part, if needed.

Therefore, after the party $2\frac{1}{2}$ pizzas were left over.

Proper/Improper Fraction

If the numerator of a fraction is less than than its denominator, we say it is a *proper fraction*. The quantity represented by a proper fraction is always smaller than the whole.

If the numerator of a fraction is more than or equal to its denominator, we say it is an *improper fraction*. The quantity represented by an improper fraction is greater than or equal to the whole.

Mixed Number

A *mixed number* consists of an integer and an improper fraction.

An improper fraction can be written as a mixed number by dividing the numerator by the denominator:

$$\text{Denominator} \longrightarrow 7\overline{)25} \begin{array}{l} 3 \leftarrow \text{Integer} \\ \\ 4 \leftarrow \text{Numerator} \end{array}$$

$$\frac{25}{7} = 3\frac{4}{7}$$

Example 3.10

During PE class, the teacher grouped the students and asked each group to run a total of 15 laps around the track. To do this all members of the team have to run at least one lap, and when adding together the distances that they ran, they needed to have at least 15 whole laps.

Aldo, Ben, Charlie, and Donna are on the same team. So far Aldo ran $3\frac{3}{4}$ laps, Ben ran $2\frac{1}{3}$ laps, Charlie ran $3\frac{1}{2}$ laps, and Donna ran $1\frac{2}{3}$.

How many more laps do they need to run?

Solution

Let's add together the number of laps they all ran. Since we are given mixed numbers, we can add the integer portions of the mixed numbers and the fractional parts, and then combine everything together.

Let's start by adding the fractional parts together. The fractions have denominators 4, 3 and 2, which have LCM 12, so we'll use that as our common denominator.

$$
\begin{aligned}
\frac{3}{4} + \frac{1}{3} + \frac{1}{2} + \frac{2}{3} &= \frac{3 \times 3}{4 \times 3} + \frac{1 \times 4}{3 \times 4} + \frac{1 \times 6}{2 \times 6} + \frac{2 \times 4}{3 \times 4} \\
&= \frac{9}{12} + \frac{4}{12} + \frac{6}{12} + \frac{8}{12} \\
&= \frac{9 + 4 + 6 + 8}{12} \\
&= \frac{27}{12} \\
&= 2\frac{3}{12} \\
&= 2\frac{1}{4}
\end{aligned}
$$

The integer portions of the mixed numbers add up to $3 + 2 + 3 + 1 = 11$ and, since the fractional parts of the mixed numbers add up to $2\frac{1}{4}$, we can say they have run so far $13\frac{1}{4}$ laps.

Their goal is to run for at least 15 laps, so to find out how many more laps they need to run we need to subtract $13\frac{1}{4}$ from 15. To subtract a mixed number from an integer, we can start by subtracting the integer portion, then subtract the fractional portion from what we have left. We have

$$
15 - 13\frac{1}{4} = 2 - \frac{1}{4} = \frac{8}{4} - \frac{1}{4} = \frac{8-1}{4} = \frac{7}{4} = 1\frac{3}{4},
$$

so they still need to run $1\frac{3}{4}$ laps.

3.2 Quick Response Questions

Problem 3.1 Carrie has 20 math questions to do for her homework. If she has already completed 7 problems, what fraction of the questions has Carrie solved?

(A) $\dfrac{7}{20}$

(B) $\dfrac{7}{13}$

(C) $\dfrac{13}{20}$

(D) $\dfrac{20}{7}$

Problem 3.2 What is the missing numerator in the following addition?

$$\frac{3}{15} + \frac{8}{15} = \frac{\Box}{15}$$

Problem 3.3 Consider the 4 shaded squares out of 16 total in the diagram below.

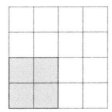

Which of the following fractions does NOT describe the fraction of the 16 squares that are shaded?

(A) $\dfrac{2}{8}$

(B) $\dfrac{4}{16}$

(C) $\dfrac{1}{2}$

(D) $\dfrac{1}{4}$

Problem 3.4 The fraction $\dfrac{8}{30}$ can be simplified to $\dfrac{4}{\square}$. What is the missing denominator?

Problem 3.5 What is $\dfrac{1}{5} + \dfrac{1}{6}$?

(A) $\dfrac{5}{16}$

(B) $\dfrac{11}{60}$

(C) $\dfrac{11}{15}$

(D) $\dfrac{11}{30}$

Problem 3.6 What is the missing numerator in the following addition?

$$\frac{1}{4} + \frac{1}{6} = \frac{\square}{12}$$

Problem 3.7 What is the missing denominator in the following multiplication?

$$\frac{3}{4} \times \frac{1}{2} = \frac{3}{\square}$$

Problem 3.8 What is $\frac{2}{11} \div \frac{3}{4}$?

(A) $\frac{6}{44}$

(B) $\frac{33}{8}$

(C) $\frac{8}{33}$

(D) $\frac{3}{22}$

Problem 3.9 Write the improper fraction $\dfrac{25}{6}$ as a mixed number.

(A) $\dfrac{1}{6}$

(B) $6\dfrac{1}{25}$

(C) $5\dfrac{1}{6}$

(D) $4\dfrac{1}{6}$

Problem 3.10 Which of the following is NOT equal to $\dfrac{4}{5}+\dfrac{4}{6}$?

(A) $1\dfrac{14}{30}$

(B) $1\dfrac{22}{15}$

(C) $\dfrac{22}{15}$

(D) $1\dfrac{7}{15}$

3.3 **Practice**

Problem 3.11 Ross bought an apple pie and sliced into 10 equal portions.

Ross ate 2 slices of pie, his mom ate 3 slices, and his dad ate 4 slices.

What fraction of the pie is left?

Problem 3.12 Tatiana bought a bar of chocolate and split it into 8 pieces of equal size.

She ate 3 pieces of chocolate before lunch, and 2 pieces after dinner.

What fraction of the chocolate has Tatiana eaten so far?

Problem 3.13 Gordie cut 7 sheets of paper in 8 pieces each.

He wrote the letters on the alphabet in the smaller pieces of paper, one letter per piece of paper. He then wrote the digits 0 through 9 in some of the remaining pieces of paper, again one digit per piece of paper.

How many sheets of paper does he have left? Remember 8 pieces of paper make for one whole sheet of paper. Give your answer as an improper fraction and a mixed number. Make sure to simplify your answers.

Problem 3.14 Calculate the following:

(a) $\dfrac{8}{11} + \dfrac{4}{11}$

(b) $\dfrac{7}{15} - \dfrac{2}{15}$

(c) $\dfrac{8}{9} + \dfrac{7}{9}$

Problem 3.15 Todd had a large bag of rice. He split the bag into 15 equal sized bags. Of these smaller bags, he sold 4, gave away 3, and cooked 2.

What fraction of the large bag does he have left?

Problem 3.16 Roy and Tracy each got a big bag of jelly beans, and each big bag has the same number of jelly beans. Roy split his jelly beans evenly into 7 smaller bags, and Tracy split her jelly beans evenly into 14 smaller bags.

During lunch Roy ate 3 of his smaller bags of jellybeans and Tracy ate 5 of her smaller bags of jelly beans.

Who ate more jelly beans? By how much more (in terms of fraction of a big bag)?

Problem 3.17 Brenda and Stacy bought apple pies. Brenda sliced hers into 12 equal slices, and Stacy sliced hers into 9 equal slices.

After eating some of their pies, they both had $\frac{2}{3}$ of their pies left.

How many slices of pie do Brenda and Stacy have left?

Problem 3.18 As part of a homework assignment, Eustace needs to take 150 pictures of food. So far he has taken 65 pictures.

What fraction of his assignment does Eustace have yet to complete?

Problem 3.19 Write 3 equivalent fractions for each of the following:

(a) $\dfrac{2}{7}$

(b) $\dfrac{6}{24}$

(c) $\dfrac{4}{10}$

Problem 3.20 Dustin had some chocolate bars of the same size. On Monday he ate $\dfrac{2}{3}$ of a bar, on Tuesday he ate $\dfrac{3}{7}$ of a bar, and on Wednesday he ate $\dfrac{16}{21}$ of a bar.

How much chocolate did he eat from Monday through Wednesday?

Problem 3.21 Harvey decided to paint the fence in his backyard. Two days ago he painted $\dfrac{5}{12}$ of the fence, a day ago he painted $\dfrac{1}{3}$ of the fence, and today he painted $\dfrac{1}{6}$ of the fence.

What fraction of the fence does Harvey still have to paint?

Problem 3.22 Calculate the following

(a) $\dfrac{13}{16} + \dfrac{3}{4} - \dfrac{3}{8}$

(b) $\dfrac{4}{9} + \dfrac{5}{6} - \dfrac{5}{12}$

(c) $\dfrac{11}{15} + \dfrac{12}{25} + \dfrac{13}{10}$

Problem 3.23 Patty has 25 colored pencils. $\frac{2}{5}$ of her color pencils are blue, and $\frac{2}{3}$ of the rest are red.

(a) How many of her pencils are blue?

(b) What fraction of her pencils are red? How many pencils is that?

(c) What fraction of her color pencils are not blue nor red? How many pencils is that?

Problem 3.24 Darcey spent $\frac{2}{7}$ of her paycheck buying Christmas gifts, and $\frac{1}{5}$ of her paycheck in groceries.

She then spent $\frac{7}{9}$ of the remaining money paying rent. What fraction of her paycheck did Darcy spend paying rent?

Problem 3.25 Calculate the following:

(a) $2 \times \dfrac{5}{7}$

(b) $\dfrac{7}{25} \times \dfrac{5}{28}$

(c) $\dfrac{7}{12} \times \dfrac{3}{14}$

Problem 3.26 Carmen decided to paint the walls of her apartment. She was able to paint $\dfrac{2}{5}$ of her walls before some friends came to visit her. The next day she painted $\dfrac{1}{2}$ of what was left to paint.

What fraction of her walls is still left to paint?

Problem 3.27 Calculate the following:

(a) $\dfrac{8}{15} \div \dfrac{3}{5}$

(b) $\dfrac{10}{21} \div \dfrac{2}{7}$

(c) $\dfrac{80}{81} \div \dfrac{5}{3}$

Problem 3.28 Larson is making smoothies. To make his smoothies extra sweet, Larson adds $\dfrac{1}{8}$ of a cup of syrup to each smoothie.

If Larson has $\dfrac{25}{4}$ cups of syrup, how many smoothies can he make?

Problem 3.29 The bank is open for 8 hours each day. So that they can take breaks, security guards at the door change every $\frac{2}{3}$ of an hour.

How many times would security guys change during one day?

Problem 3.30 Larry and Tim found $6\frac{3}{4}$ leftover pizzas in their fridge. It is too much pizza for the two of them so they plan on inviting some friends over to share.

If they estimate that each person would eat $\frac{3}{8}$ of a pizza, how many people (including Larry and Tim) could come over and have some pizza?

Problem 3.31 Write each improper fraction as a a mixed number. Simplify your answer.

(a) $\frac{30}{7}$

(b) $\frac{72}{27}$

(c) $\dfrac{81}{16}$

Problem 3.32 As part of a competition, a team of 4 people have to go through a maze with obstacles holding a bucket of water. Once all 4 team members finish the maze they pool their water together. The winner team is the one with the most water.

Alec, Brie, Charles, and Diane were able to finish the maze with $2\dfrac{1}{3}$, $3\dfrac{1}{2}$, $1\dfrac{5}{6}$, and $3\dfrac{2}{3}$ liters of water, respectively. How much water did their team collect?

Problem 3.33 Yolanda wants to bake chocolate cakes. Her recipe calls for $2\dfrac{1}{2}$ cups of flour, $3\dfrac{1}{4}$ cups of sugar, and $\dfrac{1}{3}$ cups of cocoa powder.

In her pantry she has 25 cups of flour, 30 cups of sugar, and 3 cups of cocoa powder. How many cakes can she bake?

Problem 3.34 Florence got $1800 for her birthday. She spent $\dfrac{1}{6}$ of the money on a video game console, and $\dfrac{2}{9}$ of the money on clothes.

How much money does she have left?

Problem 3.35 Esteban and Patrick decided to go to the movies, and each of them got a large bucket of popcorn.

Before the movie started Esteban ate $\frac{5}{12}$ of his popcorn. By the end of the movie he had $\frac{3}{8}$ of his popcorn left.

(a) Before the movie Patrick ate twice as much popcorn as Esteban. What fraction of his popcorn did he have left after this?

(b) What fraction of his popcorn did Esteban eat during the movie?

(c) Patrick ran out of popcorn in the middle of the movie and went out to get one more large bucket of popcorn. By the end of the movie he had $\frac{2}{5}$ of the bucket left. How much more popcorn did he eat compared with Esteban?

4. Smaller Places

Dulcinea is working at a Chemistry laboratory. She is adding several solutions together into a big container. So far she's added 0.496 liters hydrochloric acid, 0.056 liters of sulfuric acid, and 0.8 liters of water.

How many liters is Dulcinea's solution?

The concepts introduced in this chapter directly correspond to Common Core Math Standards as shown in the following table.

4th Grade	4.NF.5, 4.NF.6
5th Grade	5.NBT.1, 5.NBT.3, 5.NBT.7

In addition to the standards above, problems and concepts in this section will help strengthen understanding of the following domains.

3rd Grade	3.NBT, 3.NF
4th Grade	4.NBT, 4.NF
5th Grade	5.NBT, 5.NF

4.1   Example Questions

Example 4.1

Sally does not like when she gets pennies and dimes as change, so she has been collecting all the pennies and dimes she's got for the past year.
She finally decided to count how much money she has in coins. She counted 346 pennies and 148 dimes. How much money does she have?

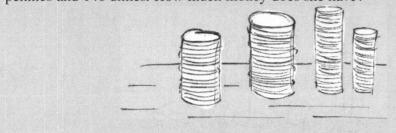

Solution

Each penny is worth 1 cent, and each dime is worth 10 cents. Since 100 cents make 1 dollar, 1 penny is equal to $\dfrac{1}{100}$ of a dollar, and 1 dime is equal to $\dfrac{10}{100} = \dfrac{1}{10}$ of a dollar.

Thus 346 pennies are worth

$$346 \times \frac{1}{100} = \frac{346}{100} = 3\frac{46}{100}$$

dollars, that is, 3 dollars and 46 cents, and 148 dimes are worth

$$148 \times \frac{1}{10} = \frac{148}{10} = 14\frac{8}{10} = 14\frac{80}{100}$$

dollars, that is, 14 dollars and 80 cents.

Therefore, in total Sally has

$$3\frac{46}{100} + 14\frac{80}{100} = 17\frac{126}{100} = 18\frac{26}{100}$$

dollars, that is, 18 dollars and 26 cents.

We are probably used to writing dollars and cents using decimal numbers, so instead of saying $18\frac{26}{100}$ dollars we usually say we have 18.26 dollars.

Decimal Numbers

Numbers with a *decimal point* are often referred to as *decimal numbers*.

Example 4.2

Roy is mixing paint of different colors. To measure the amounts of paint he needs he is using containers that can hold 1 liter, $\frac{1}{10}$ of a liter, $\frac{1}{100}$ of a liter, and $\frac{1}{1000}$ of a liter.

He mixed 4 containers of 1 liter of green paint, 3 containers of $\frac{1}{10}$ liters of red paint, 5 containers of $\frac{1}{100}$ liters of blue paint, and 7 containers of $\frac{1}{1000}$ liters of glitter.

How many liters of paint did he mix?

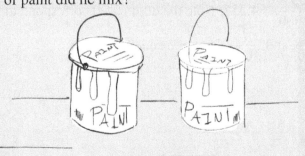

Solution

Roy mixed 4 liters of green paint, 3 tenths of a liter of red paint, 5 hundredths of a liter of blue paint, and 7 thousandths of a liter of glitter, so he mixed

$$4 \times 1 + 3 \times \frac{1}{10} + 5 \times \frac{1}{100} + 7 \times \frac{1}{1000}$$

liters of paint.

This sum is equal to

$$
\begin{aligned}
4 &+ \frac{3}{10} + \frac{5}{100} + \frac{7}{1000} \\
&= \frac{4000}{1000} + \frac{300}{1000} + \frac{50}{1000} + \frac{7}{1000} \\
&= \frac{4357}{1000} \\
&= 4\frac{357}{1000}
\end{aligned}
$$

We can rewrite this fraction using decimal numbers. Since the denominator of the fraction is 1000 and 1000 has three zeros, the number will have three digits after the decimal point.

The first digit after the decimal point represents $\frac{1}{10}$ (tenths), the second digit $\frac{1}{100}$ (hundredths), and the third represents $\frac{1}{1000}$ (thousandths). 10 hundredths are equal to 1 tenth ($\frac{10}{100} = \frac{1}{10}$), and 10 thousandths equal 1 hundredth ($\frac{10}{1000} = \frac{1}{100}$).

We have then $4\frac{357}{1000} = 4.357$. Note the digits used correspond to the numerators of the fractions $\frac{3}{10}$, $\frac{5}{100}$, and $\frac{7}{1000}$ that were added together.

Example 4.3

Renata makes chocolate desserts. She works with big chocolate tablets that can be easily broken in 10 or 100 equal pieces. She needs to be very precise with the amount of chocolate she uses for each of her creations, so she has organized in a table the number of pieces of each size that she needs for each of them.

	Pieces of size		
	1	$\frac{1}{10}$	$\frac{1}{100}$
Chocolate rabbit	0	5	6
Chocolate frog	0	7	5
Chocolate muffin	4	3	2

How many tablets of chocolate does she need for each of her creations?

Solution

As in the previous problem, we can use decimal numbers to represent the amount of chocolate needed for each of Renata's creations.

For a chocolate rabbit she needs

$$5 \times \frac{1}{10} + 6 \times \frac{1}{100} = 0.56$$

bars of chocolate, for a chocolate frog she needs

$$7 \times \frac{1}{10} + 5 \times \frac{1}{100} = 0.75$$

bars of chocolate, and for a chocolate muffin she needs

$$4 + 3 \times \frac{1}{10} + 2 \times \frac{2}{100} = 4.32$$

bars of chocolate.

> **Example 4.4**
>
> Estelle has pieces of rope of different lengths and is wondering what fraction of a meter is each of the pieces.
>
> (a) What fraction of a meter is a rope with length 0.45 meters?
> (b) What fraction of a meter is a rope with length 3.75 meters?

Solution to Part (a)

Using place values, we can see

$$0.45 = \frac{4}{10} + \frac{5}{100} = \frac{40}{100} + \frac{5}{100} = \frac{45}{100}$$

which can be simplified to

$$\frac{45}{100} = \frac{45 \div 5}{100 \div 5} = \frac{9}{20}$$

of a meter.

Solution to Part (b)

Once more, using place values we can see that

$$3.75 = 3 + \frac{7}{10} + \frac{5}{100} = \frac{375}{100}$$

which can be simplified to

$$\frac{375}{100} = \frac{375 \div 25}{100 \div 25} = \frac{15}{4}$$

of a meter, or $3\frac{3}{4}$ meters.

Remark

> We just saw that it is possible to rewrite decimal numbers as fractions using place values and decimal fractions. Well, it is also possible to do the inverse process: write a fraction as a decimal number.

Example 4.5

What is the fraction $\dfrac{74}{4}$ as a decimal number?

Solution

To write a fraction as a decimal number we just need to divide the numerator by the denominator.

When dividing $74 \div 4$, we get a quotient of 18 and a remainder of 2. To write this fraction as a decimal number, we need to go further. At this stage, when we ran out of digits in the dividend, we can place a decimal point on the quotient and add a 0 to our dividend; this allows us to continue dividing, like the following:

$$
\begin{array}{r}
18 \\
4\,\overline{)74} \\
-4 \\
\hline
34 \\
-32 \\
\hline
2
\end{array}
\quad\longrightarrow\quad
\begin{array}{r}
18. \\
4\,\overline{)74} \\
-4 \\
\hline
34 \\
-32 \\
\hline
2\,0
\end{array}
\quad\longrightarrow\quad
\begin{array}{r}
18.5 \\
4\,\overline{)74} \\
-4 \\
\hline
34 \\
-32 \\
\hline
2\,0 \\
-2\,0 \\
\hline
0
\end{array}
$$

Therefore, the fraction $\dfrac{74}{4}$ is equal to 18.5 as a decimal number.

Remark

If after adding a decimal point to the quotient and a zero to the remainder we do not get a new remainder of 0, we can add another zero an keep dividing, for example, if we do $213 \div 25$:

$$
\begin{array}{r}
8.52 \\
25 \overline{\smash{)}\,213} \\
-200 \\
\hline
13\ 0 \\
-12\ 5 \\
\hline
50 \\
-50 \\
\hline
0
\end{array}
$$

Example 4.6

What is the fraction $\dfrac{36}{11}$ as a decimal number?

Solution

If we divide as usual, adding more zeros to the remainder we get

$$
\begin{array}{r}
3.2727... \\
11 \overline{\smash{)}\,36} \\
-33 \\
\hline
3\ 0 \\
-2\ 2 \\
\hline
80 \\
-77 \\
\hline
30 \\
-22 \\
\hline
80 \\
-77 \\
\hline
3
\end{array}
$$

Note we will never be able to finish dividing, since at some point we get remainders $3, 8, 3, 8, 3, \ldots$. In cases like this we have what we call a *repeating decimal*. To indicate which are the digits that repeat we use a horizontal line over them. In this case we would say that the fraction $\dfrac{36}{11}$ is equal to $3.\overline{27}$, since the digits 27 keep repeating forever.

Repeating decimal

A *repeating decimal* is a decimal number that has a digit, or a block of digits, that repeat over and over and over again without ever ending. We use a horizontal bar over the digit (or digits) that repeat.
For example:
$$\frac{260}{37} = 7.027027027\ldots = 7.\overline{027}$$
and
$$\frac{997}{198} = 5.0353535\ldots = 5.0\overline{35}$$

Example 4.7

Dulcinea is working at a Chemistry laboratory. She is adding several solutions together into a big container. So far she's added 0.496 liters hydrochloric acid, 0.056 liters of sulfuric acid, and 0.8 liters of water.
How many liters is Dulcinea's solution?

Solution

To figure out how many liters is Dulcinea's solution we just need to add together the volumes of each of the solutions she's added to the mix.

To add decimal numbers we need to make sure to align them according to their place values. This can be done by making sure the decimal points are aligned when adding

---

them together, like the following:

$$
\begin{array}{r}
0.496 \\
0.056 \\
+ \quad 0.8 \\
\hline
\end{array}
$$

This way we add thousandths with thousandths, hundredths with hundredths, tenths with tenths, and so on. Since 0.8 has only one digit after the decimal point and the other two have three, we can add 0's to the right, as 0.8 (eight tenths) is equal to 0.800 (eight tenths, zero hundredths, zero thousandths). Then we can proceed to add the numbers as usual, making sure to keep the decimal point in the same place.

$$
\begin{array}{r}
0.496 \\
0.056 \\
+ \quad 0.800 \\
\hline
1.352
\end{array}
$$

Therefore, Dulcinea's solution is 1.352 liters.

Example 4.8

Esther wants to estimate the weight of some supplies she's working with.
  (a) She has 5 metal discs, each of them weighing 0.25 pounds. How much do they weigh together?
  (b) She has 0.7 meters of a cable that weighs 0.54 ounces per meter. How much does her cable weigh?

Solution to Part (a)

To find the total weight of all the discs we can multiply the number of discs by the weight of each disc, that is, we need to multiply 5×0.25. To multiply integers and decimals, we first ignore the decimal point and multiply as usual. Then we count the number of digits after the decimal point and keep the same number of digits after the

---

decimal point in our answer.

$$
\begin{array}{r}
5 \\
\times\ \ 25 \\
\hline
25 \\
10 \\
\hline
125
\end{array}
\qquad \longrightarrow \qquad
\begin{array}{r}
5 \\
\times\ \ 0.25 \\
\hline
25 \\
10 \\
\hline
1.25
\end{array}
$$

Therefore, all 5 discs together weigh a total of 1.25 pounds.

Solution to Part (b)

Once again, to figure out the total weight we need to multiply. This time we want to find 0.7×0.54.

We will proceed exactly as in the previous example, only this time we will add the number of digits after the decimal point of each of the numbers to decide how many digits must be after the decimal point in our answer.

$$
\begin{array}{r}
7 \\
\times\ \ 54 \\
\hline
28 \\
35 \\
\hline
378
\end{array}
\qquad \longrightarrow \qquad
\begin{array}{r}
0.7 \\
\times\ \ 0.54 \\
\hline
28 \\
35 \\
\hline
0.378
\end{array}
$$

Therefore, her cable weighs 0.378 ounces.

Example 4.9

Lisa has two sticks, each 3.6 feet long. She wants to cut them in smaller pieces.
  (a) She plans on cutting one of the sticks in 3 equal pieces. How long will each of the pieces be?
  (b) She wants to cut the other stick in pieces that are 0.12 feet long. How many pieces would she get?

Solution to Part (a)

To find the length of each of the pieces we need to divide $3.6 \div 3$.

To divide a decimal number by an integer we will proceed almost as usual. As the first step we will place the decimal point right above the place where it is already, as follows:

$$
3 \overline{)3.6} \quad \longrightarrow \quad
\begin{array}{r}
1.2 \\
3 \overline{)3.6} \\
-3 \\
\hline
0\,6 \\
-6 \\
\hline
0
\end{array}
$$

Therefore, each of the 3 pieces will be 1.2 feet long.

Solution to Part (b)

This time we want to divide $3.6 \div 0.12$, so a decimal number divided by another decimal number.

We will proceed almost as in the previous case, this time, however, we will move the decimal point of the dividend to the right as many positions as digits after the decimal point in the divisor, like so

$$
0.12 \overline{)3.6} \quad \longrightarrow \quad 12 \overline{)360.0} \quad \longrightarrow \quad
\begin{array}{r}
30.0 \\
12 \overline{)360.0} \\
-36 \\
\hline
00\,0
\end{array}
$$

Note we needed to add an extra zero since we needed to move the decimal point two places to the right but there was only one digit available.

Thus, If Lisa divides her stick into pieces of length 0.12 feet, she will get 30 pieces.

Example 4.10

Write the following repeating decimals as fractions.
 (a) $0.\overline{7}$
 (b) $0.2\overline{468}$
 (c) $0.\overline{2468}$

Solution to Part (a)

The repeating decimal $0.\overline{7}$ is equal to $0.77777\ldots$. We've seen that multiplying a decimal number by 10 moves the decimal point one place to the right, so

$$10 \times 0.\overline{7} = 7.77777\ldots$$

Notice that both $7.77777\ldots$ and $0.77777\ldots$ have *exactly the same digits* after the decimal point. If we subtract these numbers we obtain

$$
\begin{aligned}
&7.77777\ldots \\
-\,&0.77777\ldots \\
\hline
&7.00000\ldots
\end{aligned}
$$

This means

$$10 \times 0.\overline{7} - 0.\overline{7} = 7,$$

that is,

$$9 \times 0.\overline{7} = 7,$$

and so

$$0.\overline{7} = \frac{7}{9}.$$

Solution to Part (b)

We can proceed similarly as in the previous problem. We just need to be careful when we align the repeating decimals.

We have a group of 4 digits that repeat right after the decimal point, so if we want to mimic the procedure from last problem, we need to move the decimal point 4 places to the right. We can achieve this by multiplying $0.\overline{2468}$ by 10000:

$$10000 \times 0.\overline{2468} = 2468.\overline{2468} = 2468.24682468\ldots$$

Since both $2468.\overline{2468}$ and $0.\overline{2468}$ have exactly the same digits after the decimal point, if we subtract them we obtain

$$
\begin{aligned}
&2468.24682468\ldots \\
-\,&0.24682468\ldots \\
\hline
&2468.00000000\ldots
\end{aligned}
$$

This means

$$10000 \times 0.\overline{2468} - 0.\overline{2468} = 2468,$$

that is,

$$9999 \times 0.\overline{2468} = 2468,$$

and so

$$0.\overline{2468} = \frac{2468}{9999}.$$

Notice the numerator of the fraction contains exactly the same four digits that repeat and the denominator is made up with four 9's.

Solution to Part (c)

This time we have an added challenge, since not all the digits after the decimal point repeat forever.

Following the same idea as above, we want to get rid of the repeating decimals by subtracting two numbers that have exactly the same digits after the decimal point.

Multiplying $0.2\overline{468}$ by 10 gives us $2.\overline{468}$, which is a repeating decimal with repeating digits starting right after the decimal point. Multiplying $0.2\overline{468}$ by 10000 gives us $2468.\overline{468}$, which is also a repeating decimal with repeating digits starting right after the decimal point. These are the two numbers we want to subtract to get rid of the repeated decimals.

Subtracting these numbers we get to

$$2468.468468\ldots$$
$$\underline{-2.468468\ldots}$$
$$2466.000000\ldots$$

that is,

$$10000 \times 0.2\overline{468} - 10 \times 0.2\overline{468} = 2466,$$

so

$$9990 \times 0.2\overline{468} = 2466$$

and

$$0.2\overline{468} = \frac{2466}{9990}.$$

This time the numerator is not exactly the same as the repeated digits, but notice it is equal to $2468 - 2$, which is the number formed by all the digits until they start repeating minus the number formed by the digits that don't repeat. Note also that the numerator has three 9's followed by one 0, and the number had one decimal digit that does not repeat and three that did.

Remark

Looking at the last example we can see there is a simple recipe to write any repeating decimal as a fraction.

Start by counting how many digits there are after the decimal point before the group of digits that repeat, this will give the number of 0's in the denominator. Count also the number of digits that repeat, this will give the number of 9's in the denominator. For the numerator, subtract the number formed by all the digits until they start repeating and the number formed by all the digits that do not repeat.

For example:

$$0.\overline{1234} = \frac{1234}{9999},$$

$$0.1234\overline{567} = \frac{1234567 - 123}{9999000},$$

and

$$0.45\overline{432} = \frac{45432 - 45}{99900}.$$

4.2   Quick Response Questions

Problem 4.1 Frank has 5 dollar bills, 4 dimes, and 3 pennies. Written as a decimal number, how many dollars does Frank have?

Problem 4.2 Which of the following expressions correctly represents 1.23 with fractions?

(A) $1 + 2 \times \dfrac{1}{100} + 3 \times \dfrac{1}{1000}$

(B) $1 + 2 \times \dfrac{1}{10} + 3 \times \dfrac{1}{20}$

(C) $3 + 2 \times \dfrac{1}{10} + 1 \times \dfrac{1}{100}$

(D) $1 + 2 \times \dfrac{1}{10} + 3 \times \dfrac{1}{100}$

Problem 4.3 What is

$$26 + 9 \times \frac{1}{10} + 7 \times \frac{1}{100}$$

when written as a decimal number?

Problem 4.4 Which of the following represents 0.65 as a fraction?

(A) $\dfrac{13}{20}$

(B) $\dfrac{65}{1000}$

(C) $\dfrac{13}{25}$

(D) $\dfrac{3}{4}$

Problem 4.5 Which of the following represents 2.5 as a mixed number?

(A) $2\dfrac{1}{5}$

(B) $5\dfrac{1}{2}$

(C) $2\dfrac{1}{2}$

(D) $3\dfrac{1}{2}$

Problem 4.6 What is the fraction $\dfrac{12}{5}$ as a decimal number?

Problem 4.7 When written as a decimal number, the fraction $\frac{2}{9}$ has one repeating digit. What is this digit?

Problem 4.8 What is

$$0.82 + 0.28$$

when written as a decimal number?

Problem 4.9 What is 0.45×4? Give your answer as a decimal number.

Problem 4.10 What is $4.8 \div 4$?

4.3 Practice

Problem 4.11 Lois bought a soda for $3.50, chips for $1.50, and a chocolate for $1.80. She paid with 25 nickels, 25 dimes, and 13 quarters.

How much money did she receive as change?

Problem 4.12 Lester has 8 pennies, 9 dimes, 3 one dollar bills, 7 ten dollar bills, and 3 one hundred dollar bills.

How much money does Lester have?

Problem 4.13 Fill in the blanks:

(a) $0.2 = $ _____ tenths $ = $ _____ hundredths $ = $ _____ thousandths

(b) $1.5 = $ _____ tenths $ = $ _____ hundredths $ = $ _____ thousandths

(c) $2.1 = $ _____ tenths $= $ _____ hundredths $= $ _____ thousandths

Problem 4.14 What number has

(a) 5 tens, 4 ones, 0 tenths, 3 hundredths, and 9 thousandths?

(b) 7 tens, 2 ones, 5 tenths, 2 hundredths, and 6 thousandths?

(c) 1 tens, 2 ones, 0 tenths, 0 hundredths, and 1 thousandth?

Problem 4.15 Use place values to fill in the blanks:

(a) $341.074 = 3 \times 100 + \underline{\quad} \times 10 + 1 \times 1 + \underline{\quad} \times \dfrac{1}{10} + 7 \times \dfrac{1}{100} + \underline{\quad} \times \dfrac{1}{1000}$

(b) $23.076 = \underline{\quad} \times 100 + 2 \times 10 + 3 \times 1 + \underline{\quad} \times \dfrac{1}{10} \underline{\quad} \times \dfrac{1}{100} + 6 \times \dfrac{1}{1000}$

(c) $945.32 = 9 \times 100 + \underline{\quad} \times 10 + 5 \times 1 + 3 \times \dfrac{1}{10} + \underline{\quad} \times \dfrac{1}{100} + \underline{\quad} \times \dfrac{1}{1000}$

Problem 4.16 What number is equal to

(a) $3 \times 100 + 4 \times 1 + 2 \times \dfrac{1}{100} + 8 \times \dfrac{1}{1000}$

(b) $4 \times 1000 + 2 \times 10 + 3 \times 1 + 4 \times \dfrac{1}{10} + 8 \times \dfrac{1}{1000}$

(c) $3 \times 100 + 5 \times 10 + 6 \times 1 + 1 \times \dfrac{1}{100} + 2 \times \dfrac{1}{1000}$

Problem 4.17 Dorothy is baking cakes. To measure her ingredients she is using containers that can hold 1 cup, $\frac{1}{10}$ of a cup, and $\frac{1}{100}$ of a cup. For one of her creations she poured 3 times 1 cup of flour, 2 times $\frac{1}{10}$ of a cup of cocoa, and 5 times $\frac{1}{100}$ of a cup of baking powder.

How many cups has Dorothy poured on her mix so far?

Problem 4.18 Write each fraction as a decimal number.

(a) $\dfrac{39}{4}$

(b) $\dfrac{41}{50}$

(c) $\dfrac{781}{250}$

Problem 4.19 Write each decimal number as a fraction. Give your answer both as an improper fraction and as a mixed number. Make sure to simplify your answers.

(a) 2.37

(b) 0.42

(c) 3.24

Problem 4.20 Write each fraction as a decimal number.

(a) $\dfrac{12}{28}$

(b) $\dfrac{124}{333}$

(c) $\dfrac{7}{330}$

Problem 4.21 Consider the fractions $\dfrac{7}{9}$, $\dfrac{12}{99}$, and $\dfrac{123}{999}$.

(a) Write each fraction as a decimal number.

(b) What do these decimal numbers have in common?

(c) Write fractions that are equal to $0.\overline{4}$, $0.\overline{62}$, and $0.\overline{144}$.

Problem 4.22 Calculate the following:

(a) $0.28 + 3.14$

(b) $0.21 + 0.07$

(c) $5.23 + 3.25$

Problem 4.23 Calculate the following:

(a) $12.387 + 3.026$

(b) $2.52 + 3.026 + 7.105$

(c) $12.845 - 5.231 - 3.451$

Problem 4.24 Calculate the following:

(a) $8 - 2.38$

(b) $10 - 1.99$

(c) $5 - 2.45$

Problem 4.25 Owen poured 2.1 liters of water and 1.2 liters of orange juice in a large container. He stirred the container and repeated the same process two more times.

How many liters of liquid are there in Owen's container?

Problem 4.26 Write each repeating decimal as a fraction.

(a) $0.51\overline{2}$

(b) $0.23\overline{32}$

(c) $12.4\overline{737}$

Problem 4.27 Calvin had 5 ten dollar bills, 3 one dollar bills, 8 dimes, and 16 pennies in his pocket. He went to the park to climb trees and with all the jumping around he lost half of his money. He then got paid \$152 for a painting he made, and spent \$25.45 on painting supplies.

How much money does Calvin have now?

Problem 4.28 Calculate the following:

(a) 18×4.16

(b) 7.51×27

(c) 58×2.49

Problem 4.29 Marjorie needs to buy 13 wooden boards of 3.6 meters in length. They sell the wooden boards at $23.45 per meter. How much does Marjorie have to pay?

Problem 4.30 Calculate the following:

(a) 3.26×2.5

(b) 1.02×3.28

(c) 0.0026×5.64

Problem 4.31 Leslie works at a hardware store. At the store they sell cable at $20 per pound. How much would Leslie have to charge her customers if they buy

(a) 12 meters of cable that weighs 0.45 pounds per meter?

(b) 8.5 meters of cable that weighs 0.85 pounds per meter?

Problem 4.32 Calculate the following:

(a) $4.28 \div 107$

(b) $1.908 \div 53$

(c) $96.6 \div 21$

Problem 4.33 Tracy has a hose that is 179.2 meters long. If she splits it into pieces of 12.8 meters each, how many pieces would she get?

Problem 4.34 Calculate the following:

(a) $32.64 \div 0.102$

(b) $0.468 \div 0.78$

(c) $5 \div 0.12$

Problem 4.35 Emmett had 5 long bars of chocolate, each 1.8 meters long. He split each bar into pieces of 0.3 meters in length, and sold each piece for $2.45.

How much money did Emmett earn from selling all his smaller chocolate bars?

5. Prob. Solving w Fractions/Decimals

Zander, Emery, and Abby are doing some long jumps They have to run towards a mark on the floor, and jump from there as far as they can. To decide how far someone jumped there are some markings in the ground every 0.1 meters from the point where they jump. Their score will be determined by the closest marking to the point where they land after jumping.

If Zander jumped 3.42 meters, Emery jumped 4.06 meters, and Abby jumped 3.65 meters, what are their scores?

The concepts introduced in this chapter directly correspond to Common Core Math Standards as shown in the following table.

4th Grade	4.NF.3, 4.NF.4, 4.MD.1, 4.MD.2
5th Grade	5.NBT.4, 5.NF.2, 5.NF.6, 5.MD.1

In addition to the standards above, problems and concepts in this section will help strengthen understanding of the following domains.

3rd Grade	3.NBT, 3.NF, 3.MD
4th Grade	4.NBT, 4.NF, 4.MD
5th Grade	5.NBT, 5.NF, 5.MD

5.1   Example Questions

Example 5.1

Cody rode his bike for 3.5 kilometers. His sister Sally rode hers for 2500 meters.
  (a) Who rode the farthest?
  (b) How much farther did they ride? Give your answer both in meters and kilometers.

Solution to Part (a)

The three most common *metric unit* to measure distance are centimeters (cm), meters (m), and kilometers (km). If we have two distances given in different units that we want to work on (add, subtract, compare, etc.) we need first to convert all distances to the *same* unit.

Working with metric units is relatively easier than other units, since $1\,km = 1000\,m$ and $100\,cm = 1\,m$.

To change a distance from km to m, we just need to *multiply* by 1000 (that is, move the decimal point three places to the right), for example, 3.5 kilometers is the same as $3.5 \times 1000 = 3500$ meters.

Similarly, to change a distance from m to km, we just need to *divide* by 1000 (that is, move the decimal point three places to the left), for example, 2500 meters is the same as $2500 \div 1000 = 2.5$ kilometers.

Note how easy it is to go from one unit to another just by moving the decimal point to the left or right.

Now that we have the distances in the same units, we can just compare the numbers to decide which distance is greater. 3500 meters is more than 2500 meters, so Cody rode the farthest.

Solution to Part (b)

We can either compare the distances in meters or in kilometers. 3.5 is $3.5 - 2.5 = 1$ more than 2.5, so we can say Cody rode for 1 kilometer more, or equivalently, for 1000 meters more.

Example 5.2

Estelle has two strips of paper. One is blue and 45 centimeters long. The other is green and 356 millimeters long.
Which of the strips of paper is longer?

Solution

Since 100 centimeters are equivalent to 1 meter, we can say that 1 centimeter is $\dfrac{1}{100}$ of a meter. Similarly, a millimeter is $\dfrac{1}{1000}$ of a meter.

The fraction $\dfrac{1}{100}$ is equivalent to $\dfrac{10}{1000}$, so we can say that 1 centimeter is equivalent to

10 millimeters.

Thus, to convert from millimeters to meters, we just need to *divide* by 10, and to convert from meters to millimeters we need to *multiply* by 10.

Hence 45 centimeters is the same as $45 \times 10 = 450$ millimeters, and 356 millimeters is the same as $356 \div 10 = 35.6$ centimeters. From this we can see the blue paper strip is longer than the green paper strip.

> **Remark**
>
> Other metric units to measure distances are decimeter (dm), decameter (dam), and hectometer (hm). The following table summarizes the equivalence between these metric units for distance and meters.
>
> | | |
> |---:|---:|
> | millimeter (mm) | 0.001 m |
> | centimeter (cm) | 0.01 m |
> | decimeter (dm) | 0.1 m |
> | meter (m) | 1 m |
> | decameter (dam) | 10 m |
> | hectometer (hm) | 100 m |
> | kilometer (km) | 1000 m |
>
> To go from one row to the next we divide by 10 and to go to the previous row we multiply by 10.
>
> $$\text{mm} \xrightarrow{\div 10} \text{cm} \xrightarrow{\div 100} \text{m} \xrightarrow{\div 1000} \text{km}$$
> $$\text{mm} \xleftarrow{\times 10} \text{cm} \xleftarrow{\times 100} \text{m} \xleftarrow{\times 1000} \text{km}$$

Example 5.3

Which is greater, 1.25 or $1\frac{1}{5}$? ♣

Solution 1

To compare a decimal number with a fraction we can convert the decimal number into a fraction, making sure that the denominators of both numbers coincide.

1.25 is equal to $\frac{125}{100}$, and

$$1\frac{1}{5} = \frac{6}{5} = \frac{12}{10} = \frac{120}{100}.$$

Now that we have both numbers as improper fractions with the same denominator, we can just compare their numerators to decide which one is bigger. Clearly 125 is larger than 120, so we have that $1.25 = \frac{125}{100}$ is larger than $1\frac{1}{5} = \frac{120}{100}$.

Solution 2

We can also compare a fraction with a decimal number by writing the fraction as a decimal number.

As a decimal number $1\frac{1}{5} = \frac{6}{5}$ is equal to $6 \div 5 = 1.2 = 1.20$, which is smaller than 1.25.

Example 5.4

Stephen is baking some muffins. His recipe for chocolate muffins states he needs to bake the muffins for $\frac{2}{3}$ of an hour. His recipe for banana nut muffins states he needs to bake the muffins for $\frac{3}{5}$ of an hour. Stephen, however, only has access to a timer that takes the time in minutes.

(a) How many minutes should Stephen input in his timer for the chocolate muffins?

(b) What about the banana nut muffins?

Solution to Part (a)

One hour is the same as 60 minutes, so $\frac{2}{3}$ of an hour is the same as $\frac{2}{3}$ of 60 minutes, that is

$$\frac{2}{3} \times 60 = \frac{2 \times 60}{3} = 2 \times 20 = 40$$

minutes.

Solution to Part (b)

Similarly, $\frac{3}{5}$ of an hour is the same as $\frac{3}{5}$ of 60 minutes, that is,

$$\frac{3}{5} \times 60 = \frac{3 \times 60}{5} = 3 \times 12 = 36$$

minutes.

Example 5.5

Roger had a bag with 28 apples. He and his friends ate $\frac{2}{7}$ of the apples. How many apples does Roger have left?

Solution

$\frac{2}{7}$ of 28 is equal to

$$28 \times \frac{2}{7} = \frac{28 \times 2}{7} = \frac{4 \times 2}{1} = 8,$$

so Roger and his friends ate 8 apples leaving Roger with $28 - 8 = 20$ apples.

Note that, since $1 - \dfrac{2}{7} = \dfrac{5}{7}$, we can also find the number of apples *remaining* if we find $\dfrac{5}{7}$ of 28, that is,

$$28 \times \frac{5}{7} = \frac{28 \times 5}{7} = \frac{4 \times 5}{1} = 20$$

apples.

Example 5.6

George had a glass full of orange juice. He drank $\dfrac{3}{5}$ of the juice and was left with 4.8 ounces of juice in his glass. How much juice did he have originally? (Give your answer in ounces.)

Solution

Since George drank $\dfrac{3}{5}$ of his juice, he is left with $1 - \dfrac{3}{5} = \dfrac{2}{5}$ of his juice. This fraction of the juice is equal to 4.8 ounces, so we are looking for a number to fill in the blank in

$$\square \times \frac{2}{5} = 4.8$$

Since 4.8 is obtained by multiplying the number by $\dfrac{2}{5}$, we can find the number by dividing 4.8 by $\dfrac{2}{5}$. We have

$$4.8 \div \frac{2}{5} = \frac{48}{10} \div \frac{2}{5} = \frac{48}{10} \times \frac{5}{2} = \frac{48 \times 5}{10 \times 2} = \frac{48}{2 \times 2} = 12,$$

so George originally had 12 ounces of juice.

Since dividing by $\frac{2}{5}$ is the same as multiplying by $\frac{5}{2}$, to find the number we could have done

$$4.8 \div 2 \times 5 = 2.4 \times 5 = 12$$

as well.

Example 5.7

There are 60 dogs in the dog park. $\frac{2}{3}$ of the dogs are on a leash, and $\frac{1}{4}$ of the dogs that are not on a leash are playing ball. How many dogs are not on a leash and playing ball?

Solution

Out of the 60 dogs, there are

$$\frac{2}{3} \times 60 = \frac{2 \times 60}{3} = 2 \times 20 = 40$$

dogs on a leash and $60 - 40 = 20$ dogs not on a leash.

Of the 20 dogs that are not on a leash, $\frac{1}{4}$ play ball, that is, $20 \times \frac{1}{4} = 5$ dogs are not on a leash and playing ball.

Example 5.8

After spending \$350, Alec was left with $\frac{4}{9}$ of his money. How much money does Alec have left?

Solution

Since Alec was left with $\frac{4}{9}$ of his money after spending $350, $350 represents $1 - \frac{4}{9} = \frac{5}{9}$ of his money.

Thus, to find how much money he started with we can divide

$$350 \div \frac{5}{9} = 350 \times \frac{9}{5} = \frac{350 \times 9}{5} = 70 \times 9 = 630,$$

so Alec started with $630.

He has now $\frac{4}{9}$ of 630 dollars left, that is,

$$\frac{4}{9} \times 630 = \frac{4 \times 630}{9} = 4 \times 70 = 280$$

dollars.

Note that, altogether, we did

$$350 \div \frac{5}{9} \times \frac{4}{9} = 350 \times \frac{9}{5} \times \frac{4}{9} = 350 \times \frac{4}{5} = 70 \times 4 = 280.$$

Here the 9's we had on the numerator and denominator of the fractions cancel out when we multiply, which simplifies the process a little.

Example 5.9

Zander, Emery, and Abby are doing some long jumps They have to run towards a mark on the floor, and jump from there as far as they can. To decide how far someone jumped there are some markings in the ground every 0.1 meters from the point where they jump. Their score will be determined by the closest marking to the point where they land after jumping.

If Zander jumped 3.42 meters, Emery jumped 4.06 meters, and Abby jumped 3.65 meters, what are their scores?

Solution

Since Zander jumped 3.42 meters, he landed between the markings for 3.4 and 3.5 meters. Zander landed $3.42 - 3.4 = 0.02$ meters away from the 3.4 making and $3.5 - 2.42 = 0.08$ meters from the 3.5 marking. Thus the closest marking is the one for 3.4 meters.

Emery jumped 4.06 meters, so he landed between the markings for 4.0 and 4.1 meters. He landed $4.06 - 4 = 0.6$ meters from the 4.0 marking, and $4.1 - 4.06 = 0.04$ meters from the 4.1 marking. Thus the closes marking is the one for 4.1 meters.

Abby jumped 3.65 meters, so she landed between the markings for 3.6 and 3.7 meters. She landed $3.65 - 3.6 = 0.05$ meters from the 3.6 marking, and $3.7 - 3.65 = 0.05$ meters from the 3.7 marking. Since Abby's landing spot is at the same distance from the markings for 3.6 and 3.7, we'll keep the largest of the two as her score, that is, 3.7.

Rounding

Given a decimal number, the closest decimal number to this with at most one digit after the decimal point is said to be the number *rounded to the nearest tenth*.

We can also round to the nearest hundredth (two decimal places), the nearest thousandth (three decimal places), etc.

Remark

For example 3.42 is equal to 3.4 when rounded to the nearest tenth; 4.673 is equal to 4.67 when rounded to the nearest hundredth, and to 4.7 when rounded to the nearest tenth; and $4.\overline{6}$ is equal to 4.667 when rounded to the nearest thousandth, to 4.67 when rounded to the nearest hundredth, and to 4.7 when rounded to the nearest tenth.

Example 5.10

Percy has a hose that is 160 meters long. He wants to split it into smaller hoses of 12.5 meters in length.
How many smaller hoses can he get? What is the length of the piece of hose he has left over?

Solution

Since $12.5 = \dfrac{125}{10}$, we have that

$$160 \div 12.5 = 160 \div \frac{125}{10} = 160 \times \frac{10}{125} = \frac{1600}{125} = 1600 \div 125.$$

Dividing $1600 \div 125$ is equal to 12 with remainder 100, that is, this is equal to $12\dfrac{100}{125}$.

Hence Percy can get 12 hoses of length 12.5 meters and will have

$$\frac{100}{125} = \frac{800}{1000} = \frac{8}{10} = 0.8$$

meters of hose left over.

5.2 Quick Response Questions

Problem 5.1 Convert 5.23 kilometers to meters and centimeters.

(A) 523 meters, 52,300 centimeters
(B) 523,000 meters, 5,230 centimeters
(C) 5,230 meters, 5,230,000 centimeters
(D) 5,230 meters, 523,000 centimeters

Problem 5.2 Convert 145 millimeters to centimeters. Give your answer as a decimal.

Problem 5.3 Fill in the blank: 0.082 kilometers is 82 ____.

(A) decameters
(B) meters
(C) centimeters
(D) millimeters

Problem 5.4 Which of the following correctly orders $\frac{2}{5}$, 0.3, and $\frac{1}{3}$?

(A) $0.3 < \frac{2}{5} < \frac{1}{3}$

(B) $\frac{2}{5} < \frac{1}{3} < 0.3$

(C) $0.3 < \frac{1}{3} < \frac{2}{5}$

(D) $\frac{1}{3} < 0.3 < \frac{2}{5}$

Problem 5.5 How many minutes is $2\frac{2}{3}$ hours?

Problem 5.6 How many centimeters is $\frac{1}{4}$ of 2 meters?

Problem 5.7 Johnny buys 30 apples at the store. He puts $\frac{1}{3}$ of them in his kitchen in a bowl. How many apples does he put in his kitchen?

Problem 5.8 Sally has 60 math questions and 40 history questions as homework. She has already answered $\frac{2}{3}$ of the math questions and all of the history questions. How many questions does Sally still need to answer to complete her homework?

Problem 5.9 Which of the following correctly rounds 3.1415 to the nearest tenth?

(A) 3.14
(B) 3.1
(C) 3
(D) 3.2

Problem 5.10 Nancy has 5 meters of ribbon and uses 1.5 meters of ribbon to wrap a single present. If Nancy wraps three presents, how much ribbon does she have left over? Give your answer in meters.

5.3 **Practice**

Problem 5.11 Alexis talks during $\frac{1}{10}$ of her math class. If she talked 5 minutes less, she would only talk during $\frac{1}{20}$ of her class time. How long is Alexis' math class?

Problem 5.12 Johnny spent $\frac{2}{3}$ of his money on a pen and a calculator. The calculator cost 3 times as much as the pen. If the calculator cost \$24, how much money did he have left?

Problem 5.13 Round each of the following to the nearest integer, the nearest tenth, and the nearest hundredth.

(a) 5.369

(b) 124.263

(c) 34.0256

Problem 5.14 Mrs. Kleine made some muffins. She sold $\frac{4}{7}$ of them in the morning and $\frac{1}{6}$ of the remainder in the afternoon. If she sold 245 more muffins in the morning than in the afternoon, how many muffins did she make?

Problem 5.15 Round each of the following repeating decimals to the nearest tenth, nearest hundredth, and nearest thousandth.

(a) $4.\overline{2}$

(b) $5.\overline{28}$

(c) $6.0\overline{08}$

Problem 5.16 Convert each of the following to meters (m).

(a) 3.78 kilometers

(b) 46.52 centimeters

(c) 32.45 decameters

Problem 5.17 Lurr spent $\frac{1}{2}$ of his money on a camera and $\frac{1}{8}$ of his money on a radio. The camera cost \$120 more than the radio. How much money did he have at first?

Problem 5.18 Convert each of the following to kilometers.

(a) 1285.64 meters

(b) 569.28 hectometers

(c) 2364 centimeters

Problem 5.19 Mrs. Rishi had \$480. She used $\frac{2}{3}$ of it to buy an electric fan. She also bought a tea set for \$60. How much money does she have left?

Problem 5.20 The same way it happens with meters, in the metric system there are several units to measure volume. The most common units are liters (l) and milliliters (ml), where 1 l = 1000 ml. The rest of the units and their relationships with a liter are summarized in the table below.

milliliter (ml)	0.001 l
centiliter (cl)	0.01 l
deciliter (dl)	0.1 l
liter (l)	1 l
decaliter (dal)	10 l
hectoliter (hl)	100 l
kiloliter (kl)	1000 l

Use the table to convert each of the following volume measurements to liters.

(a) 98465.2 milliliters

(b) 3.64 kiloliters

(c) 65.235 hectoliters

Problem 5.21 For each of the following pairs of numbers choose the one that is the smallest.

(a) $\dfrac{29}{13}$ and 2.23.

(b) 6.78 and $\dfrac{81}{12}$.

(c) $4\dfrac{7}{16}$ and 4.53.

Problem 5.22 Declan bought 27 sandwiches for $160. How much did he pay for each sandwich? Give your answer in dollars rounded to the nearest cent.

Problem 5.23 Clara spent $\frac{2}{5}$ of her money and had $60 left. How much money did she have at first?

Problem 5.24 From each of the following pairs of numbers choose the one that is the largest.

(a) $\frac{34}{99}$ and $0.\overline{42}$.

(b) $\frac{28}{999}$ and $0.\overline{28}$.

(c) $\frac{12}{33}$ and $0.\overline{12}$.

Problem 5.25 Paul has a container with 12 liters of green potion. He wants to fill small vials with 0.35 liters of potion.

(a) How many vials can he fill?

(b) How much potion will he have left in the original container after he fills as many vials as possible? Give your answer in liters rounded to the nearest tenth.

Problem 5.26 Steve has 5 wooden boards, each 2.94 meters long. He wants to split each board into boards with the same width as the original and 0.45 meters in length.

How many pieces of 0.45 meters in length can he obtain by doing this?

Problem 5.27 Dolly has a length of rope of 23.5 meters. From this she wants to cut pieces that are 55 centimeters in length.

If she cuts as many pieces as possible, how many pieces would she obtain? How much rope will she have left over?

Problem 5.28 There are 50 kumquats in a box. $\dfrac{3}{10}$ of them are rotten. How many of the kumquats are not rotten?

Problem 5.29 After spending $30 on a dress, Maria had $\dfrac{3}{8}$ of her money left. How much money did she have at first?

Problem 5.30 $\dfrac{4}{7}$ of a group of children are boys, and the rest are all girls. If there are 18 more boys than girls, how many children are there altogether?

Problem 5.31 A tank is $\dfrac{4}{5}$ full of punch. If 40 gallons more of punch are needed to fill the tank completely, what is the capacity of the tank?

Problem 5.32 There are 1400 students in a school. $\dfrac{1}{4}$ of the students wear glasses. $\dfrac{2}{7}$ of those who wear glasses are boys. How many boys in the school wear glasses?

Problem 5.33 Lohan made some tarts. She sold $\frac{3}{5}$ of them in the morning and $\frac{1}{4}$ of the remainder in the afternoon. If she had 300 tarts left, how many tarts did she make?

Problem 5.34 Alexis spent $\frac{1}{3}$ of her pocket money on a toy car and $\frac{2}{3}$ of the remainder on a toy robot. She had $20 left. How much did she spend altogether?

Problem 5.35 When the same whole number was added to both the numerator and denominator of $\frac{2}{5}$, the new fraction's value was $\frac{2}{3}$. What number was added?

6. Problem Solving with Divisibility

On her homework, Bic needed to multiply 123454321 by 9. Right before she turned in the homework, she realized one of the digits of her answer accidentally got erased:

111□088889.

Can you help Bic quickly fill in the missing digit?

The concepts introduced in this chapter go beyond 3rd, 4th, and 5th Common Core Math Standards. Problems and concepts in this section will help strengthen understanding of the following domains.

3rd Grade	3.OA, 3.NBT
4th Grade	4.OA, 4.NBT
5th Grade	5.NBT

6.1 Example Questions

Example 6.1

On her homework, Bic needed to multiply 123454321 by 9. Right before she turned in the homework, she realized one of the digits of her answer accidentally got erased:

$$111\square088889.$$

Can you help Bic quickly fill in the missing digit?

Solution

Since the number $111\square088889$ was obtained by multiplying 123454321 by 9, it must be true that the sum of its digits is a multiple of 9.

The sum of the digits that were not erased is

$$1+1+1+0+8+8+8+8+9 = 44.$$

Of all multiples of 9, the ones closest to 44 are 36 and 45. If the sum of the digits of the number was 36, the missing digit would be $36 - 44 = 12$, but that is not a single digit so this cannot be the sum. If the sum was 45, the missing digit would be $45 - 44 = 1$, so this must be digit that got erased.

Example 6.2

John's favorite number is 2 and he starts writing down the numbers that only use 2 in their digits:

$$2, 22, 222, 2222, 22222, 222222, \ldots$$

(a) Since $2 \times 2 = 4$, John also likes the number 4. Are any of these numbers divisible by 4? If so, which ones?

(b) Are any of these numbers divisible by 3? If so, which ones?

Solution to Part (a)

The rule for divisibility by 4 says that a number is divisible by 4 if its last two digits form a number that is a multiple of 4.

2 is clearly not a multiple of 4. Except for 2, all of John's numbers end in 22. 22 is not a multiple of 4, so none of these could be a multiple of 4.

Solution to Part (b)

The rule for divisibility by 3 says that a number is a multiple of 3 if the sum of its digits is a multiple of 3.

Since all numbers are formed by using the digit 2 repeatedly, the sum of their digits is equal to 2 times the number of digits it has. So, for one of this sums to be a multiple of 3, we need to have a multiple of 3 number of digits.

Therefore out of these numbers, 222, 222222, 222222222, etc. are divisible by 3, that is, every third number on John's list.

Example 6.3

How many 3-digit integers are divisible by 47?

Solution

The largest 3-digit number is 999. Since $999 \div 47 \approx 21.3$, there are 21 multiples of 47 that are less than or equal to 999 ($47 \times 1 = 27$, $47 \times 2 = 94$,..., $47 \times 21 = 987$). From these, we want to remove all the numbers that have less than 3 digits.

The largest 2-digit number is 99, and since $99 \div 47 \approx 2.1$, there are 2 multiples of 47 that are less than or equal to 99. So out of the 21 multiples of 47 that we found have at most 3 digits, 2 have less than 3 digits.

Therefore there are $21 - 2 = 19$ multiples of 47 that have exactly 3 digits.

Example 6.4

What is the smallest 4-digit number divisible by 45?

Solution 1

Since the number is a multiple of 5, its last digit must be 0 or 5, and since the number is a multiple of 9, the sum of its digits must be a multiple of 9.

To make sure the number is as small as possible, we want to use digits that are as small as possible.

If the last digit of the number is 0, the smallest multiple of 9 we can make by adding three single digit numbers and 0 is $1 + 0 + 8 + 0 = 9$, and the smallest number we can make with these digits is 1080.

If the last digit of the number is 5, the smallest multiple of 9 we can make by adding three single digit numbers and 5 is $1 + 0 + 3 + 5 = 9$, and the smallest number we can make with these digits is 1035.

1035 is smaller than 1080, so the number we are looking for is 1035.

Solution 2

The smallest 4-digit number is 1000. A number is a multiple of 5 and 9 if it is a multiple of 45 (since 5 and 9 do not have any common prime factors).

Since $1000 \div 45 = 22$ with remainder 10, $45 \times 22 = 990$ is the largest 3-digit multiple of 45, and $45 \times 23 = 1035$ is the smallest 4-digit multiple of 45.

Example 6.5

Abby and Bruce each pick a digit from 0 to 9. They form a 5-digit number starting with Abby's digit and ending with Bruce's digit. The middle three digits are 121 in that order.
If this 5-digit number is divisible by 36, what numbers could Abby and Bruce have chosen?

Solution

The number 36 can be factored like $2^2 \times 3^2$. So, a number is divisible by 36 if it is divisible by $2^2 = 4$ and $3^2 = 9$.

For the number to be a multiple of 4 its last two digits must form a number that is a multiple of 4. Since the second to last digit of the number is 1, the last digit can be 2, or 6.

Since the number is supposed to be a multiple of 9, the sum of its digits must also be a multiple of 9.

If the last digit of the number is 2, the sum of the digits we have so far is $1 + 2 + 1 + 2 = 6$; the closest multiple of 9 that is 6 or more is 9, so the remaining digit should be $9 - 6 = 3$, giving the number 31212.

If the last digit of the number is 6, the sum of the digits we have so far is $1 + 2 + 1 + 6 = 10$; the closest multiple of 9 that is 10 or more is 18, so the remaining digit should be $18 - 10 = 8$, giving the number 81216.

Therefore there are two possible answers: Abby chose 3 and Bruce chose 2, or Abby chose 8 and Bruce chose 6.

Example 6.6

How many numbers smaller than 1000 are divisible by 25 but not by 125?

Solution

We can start by finding how many numbers smaller than 1000 are multiples of 25, and how many are multiples of 125.

The largest number that is smaller than 1000 is 999. Dividing 999 by 25 and 125 we get $999 \div 25 = 39.96$ and $999 \div 125 \approx 7.99$, so there are 39 multiples of 25 that are smaller than 1000 ($25 \times 1 = 25, 25 \times 2 = 50, ..., 25 \times 39 = 975$) and 7 multiples of 125 that are smaller than 1000 ($125 \times 1 = 125, ..., 125 \times 7 = 875$).

Observe that $125 = 5 \times 25$, so 125 itself is a multiple of 25. This means all multiples of 125 are also multiples of 25. So the 7 multiples of 125 that we found are also on the list of multiples of 25.

Since we do not want multiples of 125, we are left with $39 - 7 = 32$ numbers that are multiples of 25 and are not multiples of 125.

Example 6.7

Larry keeps forgetting the 4-digit PIN he set for his bank account. To make sure not to forget it again, he decided to generate a PIN using his favorite numbers: 3, 5, and 11. He set up his PIN to be the 4-digit number that uses only the digits 3 and 5, starts with 35, and is divisible by 11. What is Larry's PIN?

Solution

Since the 4-digit number starts with 35, it looks like $\overline{35ab}$ for some digits a and b.

Using the digits 3 and 5 for a and b we can make the numbers 3533, 3535, 3553 and 3555. The number is a multiple of 11, so the alternating sum of its digits should also be a multiple of 11. The alternating sums of the digits of these numbers are $3-3+5-3=2$, $5-3+5-3=4$, $3-5+5-3=0$, and $5-5+5-3=2$. Of these, the only alternating sum of digits that is a multiple of 11 is $0 = 11 \times 0$, which corresponds to the number 3553, so that is Larry's PIN.

Example 6.8

What is the smallest positive integer that is made up entirely of 1's and 3's, at least one of each, and is divisible by 3?

Solution

A number is divisible by 3 if the sum of its digits is divisible by 3. We want the number to be as small as possible, so we should use the least number of digits possible.

For a number that uses only 1's and 3's as its digits, the sum of its digits will be equal to the number of 1's used plus three times the number of 3's used. Note that if a number is already a multiple of 3, we can attach more 3's to it and the result would still be a multiple of 3. The smallest possible sum we can obtain by adding just 1's to get a multiple of 3 is $1+1+1$, so the number we are looking for must have three 1's and one 3 (since we wanted at least one of each digit).

Using these digits the smallest number we can form is 1113, so this is the number we are looking for.

Example 6.9

How many positive multiples of 3 smaller than 10000 use only the digits 1 and 2?

Solution

Numbers that are smaller than 10000 have at most 4 digits. Since we want the numbers to be multiples of 3, we want to make sure that the sum of their digits is a multiple of 3.

The 1-digit numbers we can make with 1's and 2's are only 1 and 2, neither of which is divisible by 3.

The only way to add up to 3 using two digits is $1 + 2 = 3$, so there are two 2-digit numbers that are multiples of 3: 12 and 21.

Using three digits, we can add up to a multiple of 3 by doing $1 + 1 + 1 = 3$ or $2 + 2 + 2 = 6$, so there are two 3-digit numbers that are multiples of 3: 111 and 222.

Using 4 digits, we can add to a multiple of 3 by doing $1 + 1 + 2 + 2$. Using this digits we can create the numbers 1122, 1212, 1221, 2112, 2121, and 2211, so there are 6 four-digit numbers that are multiples of 3.

Altogether we have $2 + 2 + 6 = 10$ numbers smaller than 10000 that use only the digits 1 and 2 and are multiples of 3.

Example 6.10

What is the smallest seven-digit number that has only two different digits and is divisible by 30?

Solution

Since $30 = 2 \times 3 \times 5$, we need the number to be a multiple of 2, a multiple of 3, and a multiple of 5.

Because the number is a multiple of both 2 and 5, its last digit must be 0. So that is one of the digits we'll use.

To make the number as small as possible we want to use the smallest possible digits. We are already using 0, so for the other digit we can use 1. The first digit cannot be 0, so it must be a 1.

To make sure the number is a multiple of 3, we need the sum of its digits to be a multiple of 3. If we are using only 1's and 0's, the sum of the digits of the number is equal to the number of 1's used. This means we need either three 1's, or six 1's, and the rest are 0's. We are looking for the smallest possible number, so we should use the least number of

---

1's possible. So, the number must have three 1's and four 0's, the first digit being 1 and the last digit being 0.

Under this conditions the smallest number we can make is 1000110.

6.2 Quick Response Questions

Problem 6.1 A number is multiplied by 5. The last digit of the result:

(A) could be any digit.
(B) must be a 5.
(C) could be a 0 or a 5.
(D) must be a 0.

Problem 6.2 Which of the following digits could be the last digit of a number divisible by 2?

(A) 7
(B) 8
(C) 9
(D) All of the above.

Problem 6.3 Which of the following digits could be the last digit of a number divisible by 3?

(A) 7
(B) 8
(C) 9
(D) All of the above.

Problem 6.4 How many numbers from 1 to 99 are divisible by 7?

Problem 6.5 What is the smallest 4-digit number that is divisible by 9?

Problem 6.6 Consider the 3-digit number 2□8 missing its tens digit. If the number is divisible by 3, how many possibilities for the missing digit are there?

Problem 6.7 Consider the 3-digit number 2□8 missing its tens digit. If the number is divisible by 11, how many possibilities for the missing digit are there?

Problem 6.8 How many 2-digit numbers are divisible by 11 but not by 2?

Problem 6.9 How many multiples of 5 from 1 to 1000 use only the digits 0 and 5?

Problem 6.10 What is the smallest 4-digit multiple of 3 that only uses the digits 1 and 2?

6.3 Practice

Problem 6.11 The number 24□68, which is missing one digit, is divisible by 9. What is the missing digit?

Problem 6.12 The number 357□2, which is missing one digit, is divisible by 3 but not by 9. What could be the value of the missing digit?

Problem 6.13 Consider the numbers

$$2, 23, 232, 2323, 23232, \ldots, \underbrace{23\ldots32}_{23 \text{ digits}}.$$

(a) How many of them are divisible by 4?

(b) How many of them are divisible by 8?

Problem 6.14 How many 2-digit numbers are divisible by 17?

Problem 6.15 How many 3-digit numbers are divisible by 33?

Problem 6.16 How many 4-digit numbers are divisible by 44?

Problem 6.17 What is the smallest 4-digit number divisible by 37?

Problem 6.18 What is the largest 4-digit number divisible by 37?

Problem 6.19 What is the smallest number larger than 5000 that is divisible by 37?

Problem 6.20 The number 1023□58□4 is divisible by 12 and has no repeated digits. What is the number?

Problem 6.21 How many 6-digit numbers of the form □7298□ are divisible by 24?

Problem 6.22 How many numbers smaller than 10000 are divisible by 18 but not by 54?

Problem 6.23 How many 4-digit numbers are divisible by 18 but not by 54?

Problem 6.24 How many numbers smaller than 10000 are divisible by 119 but not by 143?

Problem 6.25 The number □782□, which is missing its first and last digits, is divisible by 11.

How many such numbers are there?

Problem 6.26 The number □782□, which is missing its first and last digits, is divisible by 33.

How many such numbers are there?

Problem 6.27 22 is the smallest number using only the digit 2 that is divisible by 22. What is the next smallest such number?

Problem 6.28 What is the smallest positive integer that is made up entirely of 3's and 5's, at least one of each, and is divisible by 3 and 5?

Problem 6.29 What is the smallest positive integer that is made up entirely of 2's and 6's, at least two of each, and is divisible by 2 and 6?

Problem 6.30 How many positive multiples of 9 smaller than 10000 use only the digits 4 and 5?

Problem 6.31 A mystery number is the smallest number that is divisible by 9 made from four different digits, none of which are 0. What is this mystery number?

Problem 6.32 What is the smallest 6-digit number that has only two different digits, neither of them zero, and is divisible by 15?

Problem 6.33 What is the largest 7-digit number that has only two different digits and is divisible by 15?

Problem 6.34 How many 6-digit positive integers that are multiples of 6 are there that use only the digits 4 and 5?

Problem 6.35 How many numbers smaller than 1000000 have an even number of digits and are divisible by 19?

7. Problem Solving with Remainders

Mr. Applebee has an apple orchard. He usually offers tours to groups of 4, 5, or 6 people at a time.

For each tour, he has a basket with apples so that at the end of the tour he can give each of the attendees the same number of apples, and also have one apple for himself.

He usually has baskets of apples ready for when a group shows up for a tour. As he does not know in advance how many people will show up, he makes sure that the number of apples he has in a basket will work for a group of 4, 5, or 6 people.

If his baskets have the least possible number of apples in them, how many apples are there in each basket?

The concepts introduced in this chapter go beyond 3rd, 4th, and 5th Common Core Math Standards. Problems and concepts in this section will help strengthen understanding of the following domains.

3rd Grade	3.OA, 3.NBT
4th Grade	4.OA, 4.NBT
5th Grade	5.NBT

7.1   Example Questions

Example 7.1

Ricky is trying to organize his toys, so he decided to buy shelves to display his toy soldiers. Ricky can fit 14 toy soldiers in each shelf and he has 131 toy soldiers to display.
  (a) How many shelves does he need to buy?
  (b) He will start filling the shelves in order, making sure they all have 14 toy soldiers, except perhaps the last one. How many toy soldiers will there be on the last shelf?
  (c) How many more toy soldiers would he need to buy to make sure he has only full shelves?

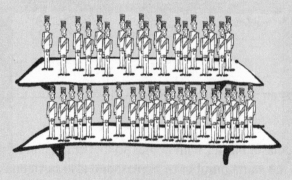

Solution to Part (a)

When we divide 131 by 14 we obtain a quotient of 9 with a remainder of 5.

This means Ricky will need to buy $9 + 1 = 10$ shelves to be able to fit all of his soldiers.

Solution to Part (b)

Since the remainder when dividing 131 by 14 is 5, the last shelf will have only 5 toy soldiers.

Solution to Part (c)

If we want the last shelf to be full, we need it to have 14 soldiers as the rest of the shelves. Since the last shelf will have 5 soldiers, Rick should buy $14 - 5 = 9$ more toy soldiers to make sure he only has full shelves.

Note that the quotient of $131 + 9 = 140$ when divided by 14 is 10 and leaves no remainder.

Example 7.2

Mrs. Chart is planning on visiting her nephews. She wants to bring candy for them, and she is pretty sure 5, 6 or 7 of her nephews will be there.
She wants to bring enough candies so that everyone gets the same number and she does not want to bring any candy back home with her.
(a) What is the least number of candies she should bring?
(b) If she wants to bring as many candies as possible, but at most 500, how many candies should she bring?

Solution to Part (a)

To make sure each of her nephews gets the same number of candy, she must bring a number of candies that is divisible by 5, 6, and 7.

The smallest number that is divisible by 5, 6, and 7, is the least common multiple of 5, 6, and 7. Since 5 and 7 are prime, and $6 = 2 \times 3$, the least common multiple of 5, 6, and 7 is $5 \times 6 \times 7 = 210$.

Thus if she brings 210 candies, she will be able to split them evenly among 5, 6, or 7 of her nephews with no problem.

Solution to Part (b)

Numbers that are divisible by 5, 6, and 7 are all multiples of the LCM of 5, 6, and 7. Thus she could bring $210 \times 1 = 210$ candies, $210 \times 2 = 420$ candies, $210 \times 3 = 630$ candies, etc.

Is she wants to bring at most 500 candies, the largest number of candies she can bring is then 420.

Example 7.3

Mr. Applebee has an apple orchard. He usually offers tours to groups of 4, 5, or 6 people at a time.
For each tour, he has a basket with apples so that at the end of the tour he can give each of the attendees the same number of apples, and also have one apple for himself.
He usually has baskets of apples ready for when a group shows up for a tour. As he does not know in advance how many people will show up, he makes sure that the number of apples he has in a basket will work for a group of 4, 5, or 6 people. If his baskets have the least possible number of apples in them, how many apples are there in each basket?

Solution

Pretend for a second that Mr. Applebee does not keep one of the apples in the basket for himself. Thus, the number of apples in the basket must be a multiple of 4, 5, and 6.

We know that a number is a multiple of 4, 5, and 6 if it is a multiple of the LCM of 4, 5, and 6, which is 60.

Hence, without keeping an apple for himself, his basket would need to have 60 apples.

Therefore, a basket with $60 + 1 = 61$ apples should do the trick.

Note if he did not want the least number of apples possible, he could have a basket with $2 \times 60 + 1 = 121$ apples, $3 \times 60 + 1 = 181$ apples, etc.

Example 7.4

Christina brought cookies to share with her friends.
When she tried to divide them evenly among 3 of her friends she had 2 cookies left over. When she tried to divide them evenly among 5 of her friends, she had 4 cookies left over. When she tried to divide them evenly among 7 of her friends, she had 6 cookies left over.
What is the least number of cookies Christina could have brought?

Solution

Since $2 + 1 = 3$, $4 + 1 = 5$, and $6 + 1 = 7$, if Christina had brought 1 more cookie, she would have been able to divide them evenly among 3, 5, and 7 people.

The smallest number that is divisible by 3, 5, and 7 is the LCM of 3, 5, and 7. Since these are prime numbers, their LCM is their product, that is, the LCM of 3, 5, and 7 is $3 \times 5 \times 7 = 105$.

Therefore, the least number of cookies Christina could have brought is $105 - 1 = 104$.

Example 7.5

Bertha is having some friends over to hang out. She prepared two trays of chicken wings with the same number of chicken wings for her friends to enjoy.

She brought one tray of chicken wings to the living room, where 6 of her friends were hanging out. Each of them ate the same number of wings and 2 wings were left on the tray.

She brought the other tray to the terrace, where 8 of her friends were hanging out. Each of them ate the same number of wings and 4 wings were left on the tray.

If each tray had at least 30 wings, what is the least possible number of chicken wings in each of the trays?

Solution

We know the number of chicken wings in each tray leaves a remainder of 2 when divided by 6, and leaves a remainder of 4 when divided by 8.

The first few numbers that leave a remainder of 2 when divided by 6 are

$$2, 8, 14, 20, 26, 32, 38, 44, \ldots$$

and the first few numbers that leave a remainder of 4 when divided by 8 are

$$4, 12, 20, 28, 36, 44, 52, 60, \ldots$$

The numbers that appear on both lists are 20, 44, etc., and since each tray had at least 30 wings, they must have come with 44 wings each.

Note that the difference between two consecutive numbers that appear on both lists is $44 - 20 = 24$, which is the LCM of 6 and 8.

Example 7.6

Ali is thinking of a number that is divisible by 6 and that leaves a remainder of 2 when it is divided by 5.

If Ali's number is between 50 and 80, what number is she thinking of?

Solution

For the number to be divisible by 6, we need for the number to be divisible by 2 and divisible by 3.

A number that is a multiple of 5 ends in 0 or 5, so a number that leaves a remainder of 2 when divided by 5 ends in $0 + 2 = 2$, or $5 + 2 = 7$.

The numbers between 50 and 80 that end in 2 or 7 are

$$52, 57, 62, 67, 72, \text{ and } 77.$$

From these, the ones that are divisible by 2 are 52, 62, and 72. From these three numbers, since $5 + 2 = 7$, $6 + 2 = 8$, and $7 + 2 = 9$, the only one that is divisible by 3 is 72.

Therefore, Ali is thinking of the number 72.

Example 7.7

Today is Thursday January 2nd of the year 2020, which is a leap year.
  (a) What day of the week will it be on January 2nd of the year 2021?
  (b) What day of the week will it be on April Fools day (April 1st) of 2020?

Solution to Part (a)

We know the days of the week repeat every 7 days: Sunday, Monday, Tuesday, Wednesday, Thursday, Friday, Saturday, Sunday, ...

Since 2020 is a leap year, it has 366 days. The remainder when dividing 366 by 7 is 2, so the day of the week after 366 days is the same as the day of the week after 2 days.

Therefore, if today is Thursday, exactly a year from now it will be two days after a Thursday, that is, Saturday.

Solution to Part (b)

In 2020 January has 31 days, February has 29 days, and March has 31 days.

February 1st is $31 - 2 + 1 = 30$ days after January 2nd. Since 30 has a remainder of 2 when divided by 7, February 1st is two day after Thursday, so Saturday.

Similarly, since March 1st is 29 days after February 1st, and 29 has a remainder of 1 when divided by 7, it will be one day after Saturday, so a Sunday.

April Fool's Day is 31 days after March 1st. Since 31 has a remainder of 3 when divided by 7, April 1st is three days after Sunday, so a Wednesday.

Leap Year

A year is said to be a *leap year* if it is divisible by 400 or it is divisible by 4 but not by 100. A leap year has an extra day (called the Leap Day) on February, so while a non-leap year has 365 days (with 28 days in February), a leap year has 366 days (with 29 days on February).

Examples of leap years are 1904, 2000, and 2020. Examples of non-leap years are 1900, 2013, and 2019.

Example 7.8

Troy's alarm clock says it is now 6:42 PM.
   (a) What number will show in the hours portion of the time exactly 50 hours from now?
   (b) What number will show in the minutes portion of the time exactly 100 minutes from now?

Solution to Part (a)

The hours of the day repeat every 12 hours in a clock that has AM/PM (12, 1, ..., 11, 12, ...).

Since dividing 50 by 12 leaves a remainder of 2, the hours portion of the time will show a number 2 hours after 6, so the alarm clock will show $6 + 2 = 8$.

Solution to Part (b)

The same way the numbers that show in the hours portion of the time repeat every 12 hours, the numbers that show in the minutes portion of the time repeat every 60 minutes $(0, 1, 2, \ldots, 59, 0, \ldots)$.

Dividing 100 by 60 leaves a remainder of 40, so the minutes shown after 100 minutes, are the same as the minutes shown after 40 minutes.

$42 + 40 = 82$, which is larger than 60, so we divide once more by 60 to find a remainder of 22. Thus, the minutes portion of the time will show 22 minutes.

Example 7.9

Consider the numbers 253 and 351.
  (a) What is the last digit of the sum $253 + 351$?
  (b) What is the sum of the last digits of 253 and 351?
  (c) How does the last digit of the sum $237 + 126$ compare with the sum of the last digits of 237 and 126?

Solution to Part (a)

The sum of 253 and 351 is 604, which has last digit 4.

Solution to Part (b)

The last digit of 253 is 3, and the last digit of 351 is 1.

The sum of 3 and 1 is 4, which coincides with the last digit of the sum of the two numbers.

Solution to Part (c)

The sum of 237 and 126 is 363, which has last digit 3.

The last digit of 237 is 7, and the last digit of 126 is 6. 6 and 7 have a sum of 13. Note this number ends in 3, as does the sum of the two numbers.

Remark

It is always true that the last digit of the sum of two numbers is the same as the last digit of the sum of the last digits of the numbers.

Example 7.10

Without dividing the numbers, find the remainder of
  (a) 34872 when it is divided by 9.
  (b) 78525 when it is divided by 11

Solution to Part (a)

The remainder upon dividing by 9 is equal to the remainder of the sum of the digits of the number.

The number 34872 has sum of digits $3 + 4 + 8 + 7 + 2 = 24$, and the number 24 has sum of digits $2 + 4 = 6$. Thus, the remainder of dividing 34872 by 9 is 6.

Note this trick works as well when we are dividing by 3.

Solution to Part (b)

The remainder upon dividing by 11 is equal t the remainder of the alternating sum of the digits of the number.

The alternating sum of the digits of 78525 is $5 - 2 + 5 - 8 + 7 = 7$. Thus, the remainder of dividing 78525 by 11 is 7.

7.2 Quick Response Questions

Problem 7.1 What is the quotient and the remainder when 100 is divided by 7?

(A) Quotient: 2, Remainder: 14
(B) Quotient: 98, Remainder: 2
(C) Quotient: 14, Remainder: 2
(D) Quotient: 13, Remainder: 9

Problem 7.2 What is the smallest number greater than 1 that leaves a remainder of 1 when divided by 7 and a remainder of 1 when divided by 10?

Problem 7.3 Which of the following lists the first few numbers that leave a remainder of 2 when divided by 3 and a remainder of 2 when divided by 4?

(A) $2, 5, 6, 8, 10$
(B) $2, 14, 26, 38, 50$
(C) $12, 24, 36, 48, 60$
(D) $14, 28, 42, 56, 70$

Problem 7.4 What is the smallest number that leaves a remainder of 6 when divided by 7 and a remainder of 7 when divided by 8?

Problem 7.5 The smallest number that leaves a remainder of 3 when divided by 5 and 4 when divided by 7 is 18. What is the next smallest number?

Problem 7.6 Frank has dinner with his aunt every 20 days. Last time they had dinner on a Thursday night. What day will it be the next time they have dinner?

(A)   Monday
(B)   Tuesday
(C)   Wednesday
(D)   Thursday

Problem 7.7 Maurice's watch has an hour, minute, and second hand. (Recall there are 60 minutes in an hour and 60 seconds in a minute.)

The second hand on his watch currently reads 42 seconds. 3690 seconds from now, what will the second hand read?

Problem 7.8 What is the last digit of the sum $13579 + 2468$?

Problem 7.9 What is the remainder when 12345 is divided by 9?

Problem 7.10 What is the remainder when 12345 is divided by 11?

7.3 Practice

Problem 7.11 Lindsey has 230 pencils that she needs to pack in boxes of 12 pencils each. She only wants full boxes of pencils, so she'll discard any left over pencils.

How many pencils will Lindsey discard?

Problem 7.12 Ramona is a florist. She was asked to make flower arrangements with 24 roses each. If she has 584 roses available, how many flower arrangements can she make? How many roses will she have left over?

Problem 7.13 Raymond needs to find the smallest possible number greater than 100 that leaves no remainder when it is divided by 4, 7, and 14. What is the number?

Problem 7.14 Paulo has a bag full or marbles. If he wanted to, he could make 10, 16 or 18 columns of marbles with the same number of marbles in each column.

What is the smallest possible number of marbles in his bag?

Problem 7.15 Mr. John is about to teach a class. He was told that there were 12 students in the class. Later someone else told him there would be 15 students in the class. He needs to bring fruit snacks for break time, and he wants to make sure that all students get the same number of fruit snacks. He also wants to keep 2 fruit snacks for himself and does not want to have any left overs.

He is not sure what is the correct number of students, so he wants to come prepared in case there are 12 or in case there are 15 students in his class. What is the least number of fruit snacks he should bring?

Problem 7.16 Find the smallest number greater than 2000 that leaves a remainder of 3 when divided by 16, 18, and 22.

Problem 7.17 A number leaves a remainder of 1 when divided by 4, a remainder of 2 when divided by 5, and a remainder of 3 when divided by 6.

What is the smallest such number?

Problem 7.18 Patrice is trying to organize her figurine collection. She tried to arrange her figurines in groups of 6, but had 4 figurines left over. She tried to arrange her figurines in groups of 8, but had 6 figurines left over. When she tried to arrange her figurines in groups of 10 she had 8 figurines left over.

What could be the least number of figurines in Patrice's collection?

194   **Chapter 7. Problem Solving with Remainders**

Problem 7.19 Becka bought a large bag of chocolates. She tried making groups of 5 chocolates, but had 3 left over. She also tried making groups of 7 chocolates, but had 4 left over.

If Becka's bag had at least 30 chocolates, what is the least number of chocolates that could have been in Becka's bag?

Problem 7.20 What is the smallest positive integer that leaves a remainder of 5 when divided by 7, and a remainder of 7 when divided by 10?

Problem 7.21 What is the smallest positive integer that is divisible by 30 and leaves a remainder of 3 when divided by 7?

Problem 7.22 A number between 70 and 100 is a multiple of 14 and leaves a remainder of 2 when divided by 6. What is the number?

Problem 7.23 What is the largest 3-digit number that leaves a remainder of 4 when divided by 6 and a remainder of 6 when divided by 8?

Problem 7.24 If November 7 of 2018 was a Wednesday, what day of the week will November 7 of 2021 be?

Problem 7.25 Five days ago was Friday. What day of the week will it be 25 days after today?

Problem 7.26 Quency visits her parents every 10 days. Her brother Bob visits their parents every 15 days.

Last time they both visited their parents on the same day it was Wednesday.

What day of the week will it be next time they both visit their parents on the same day?

Problem 7.27 Consider the number sequence

$$2, 3, 7, 1, 5, 6, 2, 3, 7, 1, 5, 6, \ldots$$

If this pattern continues, what is the 200th number in the sequence?

Problem 7.28 An alarm clock says it is now 4:31 PM. If we ignore AM/PM, what time will it be 28 hours from now?

Problem 7.29 Regina's watch says it is now 5:42. What time will be shown in Regina's watch 250 minutes from now?

Problem 7.30 The time now is 18:24. What will be the time in 30 hours and 50 minutes? Note the time is given in a 24 hour format.

Problem 7.31 What is the last digit of the sum $4235 + 49231$?

Problem 7.32 Consider the numbers 144 and 321

(a) What is the last digit of the product 144×321?

(b) What is the last digit of the product of the last digits of 144 and 321?

(c) How do the previous answers compare to each other?

Problem 7.33 Without dividing the numbers, find the remainder of the following numbers when divided by 3

(a) 23653

(b) 76485

(c) 94349

Problem 7.34 Without dividing the numbers, find the remainder of the following numbers when divided by 9

(a) 29658

(b) 76485

(c) 98379

Problem 7.35 Without dividing the numbers, find the remainder of the following numbers when divided by 11

(a) 23653

(b) 76485

(c) 94349

8. Magic Squares and Puzzles

While traveling in India, Manny got to visit the Parshvanath temple in Khajuraho. Inside the temple, the numbers 1 through 16 are arranged in a 4×4 square as shown below:

7	12	1	14
2	13	8	11
16	3	10	5
9	6	15	4

Manny learns this square has been in the temple for hundreds of years and that it is a magic square that has some additional patterns. Can you help him find the additional patterns?

The concepts introduced in this chapter go beyond 3rd, 4th, and 5th Common Core Math Standards. Problems and concepts in this section will help strengthen understanding of the following domains.

3rd Grade	3.OA, 3.NBT
4th Grade	4.OA, 4.NBT
5th Grade	5.OA, 5.NBT

8.1   Example Questions

Example 8.1

Write the numbers $1, \ldots, 9$ in the circles below so that the sum of the numbers inside opposite circles is the same.

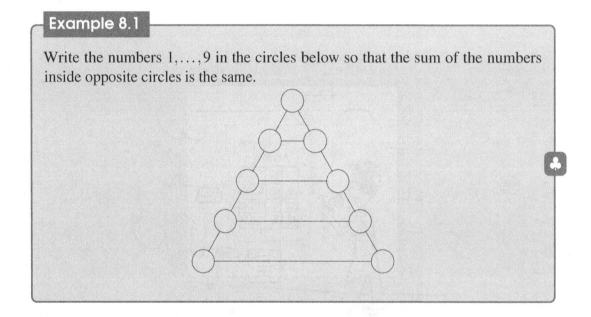

Solution 1

The numbers $1, \ldots, 9$ form an arithmetic sequence, so the first and last numbers, second and second to last numbers, etc. all add up to $1 + 9 = 10$. Thus, one way of filling the circles is to write these pairs of numbers on opposite sides. One possible arrangement could be

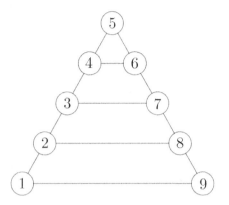

Solution 2

If we ignore the number 1, the rest of the numbers still form an arithmetic sequence. This time the first and last numbers add to $2 + 9 = 11$, so we can pair the numbers $3 + 8 = 11, 4 + 7 = 11$, and $5 + 6 = 11$. Thus, another possible solution is

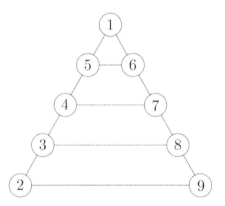

Solution 3

As we did above, if we ignore the number 9, the remaining numbers still form an arithmetic sequence with the first and last numbers adding up to $1 + 8 = 9$. So we can pair the numbers $2 + 7 = 9, 3 + 6 = 9$, and $4 + 5 = 9$. This gives us another possible solution

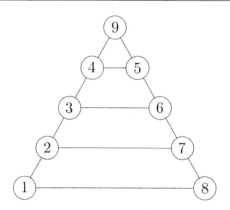

Example 8.2

Write the numbers $1, \ldots, 6$ in the circles below so that the numbers in each side of the triangle add up to 10.

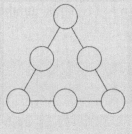

Solution

Using the numbers 1 through 6 we can add up to 10 in three different ways:

$$1 + 3 + 6, \quad 1 + 4 + 5, \quad \text{and} \quad 2 + 3 + 5,$$

so these are the triplets of numbers that will go on each of the edges.

Note that 1, 3, and 5 appear twice on these sums, so those will be the numbers in the corners.

Thus, the complete triangle with sides that add up to 10 looks like

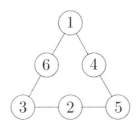

Example 8.3

Consider a 3×3 grid.

Write the numbers $1, \ldots, 9$ in the squares on the grid so that the numbers in each row, column, and diagonal add up to the same number.

Solution

The sum of all 9 numbers is $1 + 2 + \cdots + 9 = 45$. Since we want each row to add to the same number, the sum in each row must be $45 \div 3 = 15$.

Let's list all possible ways to add up to 15 using three different numbers from 1 through 9:

$$
\begin{array}{ll}
1+5+9 & 2+6+7 \\
1+6+8 & 3+4+8 \\
2+4+9 & 3+5+7 \\
2+5+8 & 4+5+6
\end{array}
$$

Notice that there are exactly different 8 ways to add up to 15 using the numbers 1 through 9, and there are also 8 different sums in the 3×3 magic square: three rows, three columns, and two diagonals.

The square in the center is involved in 4 sums: two diagonals, one row, and one column. By examining the sums we found, the only number that appears in a sum exactly 4 times is 5, so that must be the middle number.

Each of the four squares in the corners is involved in 3 sums: one row, one column, and one diagonal. Examining the sums we found, the numbers that appear in a sum 3 times are 2, 4, 6, and 8. Since we know that 5 is in the middle square and we have the sums $2+5+8$ and $4+5+6$, 2 and 8 must be in opposite corners, as well as 4 and 6.

So far our magic square looks like

2		4
	5	
6		8

At this point we can easily fill in the missing numbers in the middle squares. The complete magic square is then

2	9	4
7	5	3
6	1	8

Magic Square

A $n \times n$ grid filled with $n \times n$ numbers such that every row, column, and diagonal add to the same number is called a *Magic Square*. The sum of each row, column, and diagonal is called the *magic sum* of the Magic Square.

Remark

There are actually 8 possible ways to solve the magic square, though any of them can be obtained by reflecting or rotating the numbers in the magic square we found.

2	9	4
7	5	3
6	1	8

4	9	2
3	5	7
8	1	6

2	7	6
9	5	1
4	3	8

6	7	2
1	5	9
8	3	4

6	1	8
7	5	3
2	9	4

8	1	6
3	5	7
4	9	2

4	3	8
9	5	1
2	7	6

8	3	4
1	5	9
6	7	2

Since every other solution can be obtained by reflection or rotating our solution, we say that there is *one solution* to a 3×3 magic square.

Example 8.4

Consider a 5 × 5 grid.

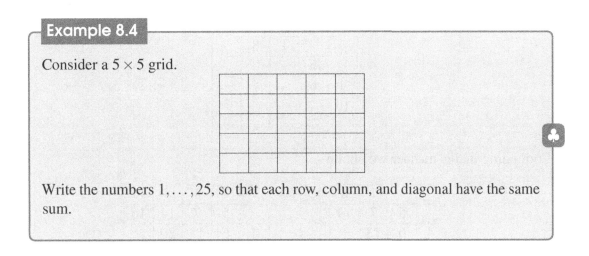

Write the numbers 1, ..., 25, so that each row, column, and diagonal have the same sum.

Solution

The following technique works for any magic square with an odd number of squares per side.

Start by placing the number 1 in the middle square of the top row.

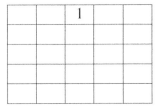

The next number will be one square up and one square to the right. Since there is no square above 1, going one square up will take us to the square at the bottom of the row where 1 is (sort of like when we play Pac-Man and exit to on the top of the screen only to arrive at the bottom of the screen).

Thus, the first 5 numbers we'll place in the grid look like

		1		
	5			
4				
				3
			2	

Since the next square is already occupied by 1, we write the next number in the square right under 5, and then proceed as before to write the next numbers, like so

		1	8	
	5	7		
4	6			
10				3
			2	9

Continuing in this manner we obtain

		1	8	15
	5	7	14	
4	6	13		
10	12			3
11		2	9	

17		1	8	15
	5	7	14	16
4	6	13	20	
10	12	19		3
11	18		2	9

So the completed 5×5 magic square looks like

17	24	1	8	15
23	5	7	14	16
4	6	13	20	22
10	12	19	21	3
11	18	25	2	9

To understand why this works let's split the magic square in two square grids, as shown below

15	20	0	5	10
20	0	5	10	15
0	5	10	15	20
5	10	15	20	0
10	15	20	0	5

$+$

2	4	1	3	5
3	5	2	4	1
4	1	3	5	2
5	2	4	1	3
1	3	5	2	4

Observe how on the grid on the left the numbers 0, 5, 10, 15, and 20 appear once in each row and in each column, and on the grid on the right the numbers 1, 2, 3, 4, and 5 appear once in each row and in each column. Furthermore, if we follow the numbers that appear in the squares we used each time we moved diagonally, we see on the left side 0, 0, 0, 0, 0 and 1, 2, 3, 4, 5 on the right side, then 5, 5, 5, 5, 5 on the left, and 1, 2, 3, 4, 5 on the right side, and so on.

Thus, the sum of each row/column on the left is 50, and the sum of each row/column on the right is 15, so the sum in each row/column of the magic square is $50 + 15 = 65$.

Remark

Unlike the solution for the 3×3 magic square, the solution to a 5×5 (or any other odd size) square is not unique. This method shows how to find *one* of many different solutions to any magic square of odd size. Of course, we can find other solutions by reflecting or rotating our solution, but not all other solutions can be obtained this way.

Example 8.5

While traveling in India, Manny got to visit the Parshvanath temple in Khajuraho. Inside the temple, the numbers 1 through 16 are arranged in a 4×4 square as shown below:

7	12	1	14
2	13	8	11
16	3	10	5
9	6	15	4

Manny learns this square has been in the temple for hundreds of years and that it is a magic square that has some additional patterns. Can you help him find the additional patterns?

(a) What is the magic sum of this magic square?

(b) Look at the four numbers in the center of the square, what is their sum?

(c) Can you find more nice sets of 4 numbers from this magic square that also add up to the magic sum?

Solution to Part (a)

The numbers 1 through 16 are used in this square. If it is a magic square, then each row, column, and diagonal should add up to $\frac{1}{4}$ of the sum of all numbers, that is,

$$(1+2+\cdots+15+16)\div 4 = 34.$$

We can verify that the rows, columns, and diagonals of this square indeed add up to 34, for example

$$2+13+8+11 = 34$$

and

$$9+3+8+14 = 34.$$

Solution to Part (b)

The four numbers in the center of the square are 13, 8, 3, and 10. We can see that their sum is $13+8+3+10 = 34$, which is the same as the magic sum of the square.

Solution to Part (c)

Look at the four numbers in the corners: 7, 14, 9, and 4. These 4 numbers add up to $7+14+9+4 = 34$.

Consider now the four bolded numbers below

7	12	1	14
2	**13**	8	**11**
16	3	10	5
9	**6**	15	**4**

Notice that they too add up to the magic sum: $13+11+6+4 = 34$. In fact, the four corners in any square that can be found inside the bigger square add up to the magic sum of 34.

Some other nice sets of 4 numbers that add up to the magic sum are

7	12	1	**14**
2	13	8	11
16	**3**	10	5
9	6	**15**	4

since $2 + 3 + 15 + 14 = 34$, and

7	**12**	1	14
2	13	8	11
16	3	10	**5**
9	6	**15**	4

since $2 + 12 + 15 + 5 = 34$.

In fact, starting from any number, the set of 4 numbers obtained by moving diagonally on the square (the same way we moved along diagonals in odd sized magic squares before) always adds up to the magic sum of 34. Because of this, we say that this 4×4 magic square is a *pan-diagonal* magic square.

Remark

> This 4×4 magic square is an instance of the *most perfect magic square*, since it is a *pan-diagonal* magic square, and the corners of every sub-square also add to the magic sum.

Example 8.6

Complete the 3×3 magic square with the numbers 6, 12, 18, 24, 30, 36, 42, 48, and 54.

(a) What is the magic sum?
(b) Is this magic square related to some other magic square we have seen?

Solution to Part (a)

The sum of all numbers is $6 + 12 + \cdots + 54 = 270$, so the sum of each row/column/diagonal should be $270 \div 3 = 90$.

Solution to Part (b)

Notice that each of the numbers is a multiple of 6. Furthermore, the numbers are 6×1, 6×2, 6×3, 6×4, 6×5, 6×6, 6×7, 6×8, and 6×9.

We already know a solution to a magic square using the numbers 1 through 9, so we can use that same solution, replacing the number with its corresponding multiple of 6:

2	9	4
7	5	3
6	1	8

$\longrightarrow$

12	54	24
42	30	18
36	6	48

Remark

Any sequence of consecutive integers can be used to fill in a magic square. Multiples of consecutive integers (which are arithmetic sequences) work as well.

Example 8.7

Consider the square grid below.

3	5	7	9	11
5	7	9	11	13
7	9	11	13	15
9	11	13	15	17
11	13	15	17	19

(a) Choose 5 different squares in the grid so that the numbers in those squares add up to 55.

(b) Can you find more than one set of 5 squares such that their numbers add up to 55?

Solution to Part (a)

It is not difficult to see that the sum of the numbers in the diagonals is equal to 55:

$$3 + 7 + 11 + 15 + 19 = 55,$$

and

$$11 + 11 + 11 + 11 + 11 = 55.$$

Solution to Part (b)

In fact, if we choose the 5 squares so that we have exactly one square of each row and one square of each column, we will obtain a sum of 55, for example:

3	**5**	7	9	11
5	7	9	11	**13**
7	9	11	13	15
9	11	13	**15**	17
11	13	**15**	17	19

gives the sum $5 + 13 + 7 + 15 + 15 = 55$ or

3	5	7	9	**11**
5	7	9	**11**	13
7	**9**	11	13	15
9	11	13	15	17
11	13	**15**	17	19

gives the sum $11 + 11 + 9 + 9 + 15 = 55$.

Example 8.8

Build a 5×5 grid like the one in the previous example, so that choosing one square from each row and column always gives the same sum.

Solution

Start by choosing any 10 numbers. For now, we'll work with the numbers $10, 11, \ldots, 19$.

Write 5 of the numbers on top of each of the 5 columns, and the remaining numbers to the left of each row. For example:

	10	12	14	16	18
11					
13					
15					
17					
19					

Then in each square of the grid write the sum of the number at the top of its column and the number at the left of its row. Proceeding like this we obtain

	10	12	14	16	18
11	21	23	25	27	29
13	23	25	27	29	31
15	25	27	29	31	33
17	27	29	31	33	35
19	29	31	33	35	37

This way, when we pick squares so that we have one from each row and one from each column and add them together, we obtain the same sum as if we add all 10 numbers that we started with: $10 + 11 + \cdots + 19 = 145$.

Example 8.9

Write the numbers 1, 2, 4, 5, 10, 20, 25, 50, and 100 in the circles below so that the product of the numbers inside opposite circles is the same.

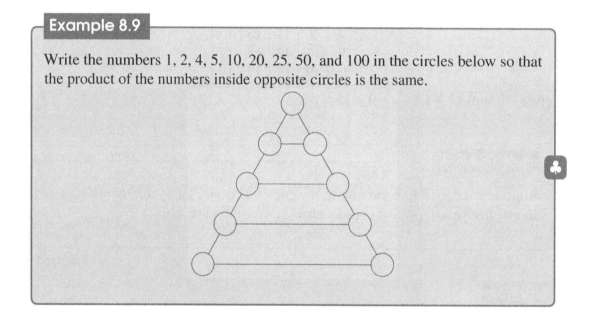

Solution

Looking carefully at the list of numbers we can see they are all the factors of 100. These factors come in pairs whose product is equal to 100: 1×100, 2×50, 4×25, 5×20, $10 \times 10 = 100$. Note 10 pairs with itself, so we'll use that for the top of the triangle.

Thus, a possible arrangement of the numbers so that the product of opposite circles is the same is

---

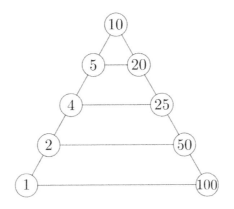

Example 8.10

Write the numbers $2, 4, 8, 16, 32, 64$ in the circles below so that the product of the numbers in each side of the triangle is equal to 512

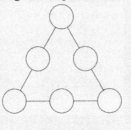

Solution

Notice that the prime factorizations of all the numbers involved in this problem use only the prime factor 2:

$$2 = 2$$
$$4 = 2 \times 2$$
$$8 = 2 \times 2 \times 2$$
$$16 = 2 \times 2 \times 2 \times 2$$
$$32 = 2 \times 2 \times 2 \times 2 \times 2$$
$$64 = 2 \times 2 \times 2 \times 2 \times 2 \times 2$$
$$512 = 2 \times 2 \times 2 \times 2 \times 2 \times 2 \times 2 \times 2 \times 2$$

Since the prime factorization of 512 has nine 2's , we want to place the numbers in the circles so that there are exactly 9 factors of 2 in each side. Thus we can start by placing the numbers 1, 2, 3, 4, 5, and 6 in the circles so that their sum is equal to 9.

There are three ways to add up to 9 using the numbers 1 through 6: $1+2+6$, $1+3+5$, and $2+3+4$. Hence our triangle with sum 9 per side looks like:

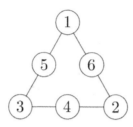

We can now replace these numbers with $2, 4, 8, \ldots$ by looking at the number of 2's in their prime factorization. Thus the triangle with product of 512 per side looks like:

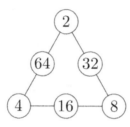

so we have $2 \times 64 \times 4 = 512$, $2 \times 32 \times 8 = 512$, and $4 \times 16 \times 8 = 512$.

8.2 Quick Response Questions

Problem 8.1 What missing number can fill in the circle below so that the numbers in each side of the triangle add up to the same number?

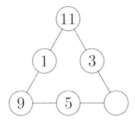

Problem 8.2 Write the numbers $5, 6, \ldots, 10$ in the circles below so that the numbers in each side of the triangle add up to 22.

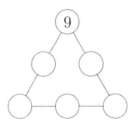

If the top corner is 9, what two numbers must be in the other corners?

(A) 7 and 10
(B) 5 and 10
(C) 5 and 7
(D) 6 and 8

Problem 8.3 What is the magic sum in the following magic square?

35	28	33
30	32	34
31	36	29

Problem 8.4 What is the sum of the three missing numbers in the following magic square?

10	3	
	7	9
6		4

Problem 8.5 Create a new magic square by adding 7 to each of the numbers in the following magic square:

2	9	4
7	5	3
6	1	8

What is the new magic sum?

(A) 15
(B) 22
(C) 29
(D) 36

Problem 8.6 Create a new magic square by multiplying each of the numbers by 7 in the following magic square:

2	9	4
7	5	3
6	1	8

What is the new magic sum?

(A) 22
(B) 105
(C) 36
(D) 90

Problem 8.7 The following magic square is missing some numbers. What is the missing number in the lower-left corner?

18			28
23	26		31
	22	32	
			24

Problem 8.8 Choose 4 squares in the grid below so that you have exactly one square in each row and exactly one square in each column.

4	8	7	11
8	12	11	15
7	11	10	14
3	7	6	10

What is the sum of the numbers in the 4 squares?

Problem 8.9 Fill in the missing circles below so that the product of opposite numbers is always the same.

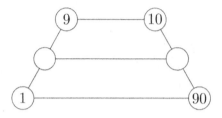

How many ways can this be done if the number on the left is a positive whole number between 1 and 9?

Problem 8.10 Fill in the missing circles below with numbers 2, 3, and 4 so that the product of each side is the same.

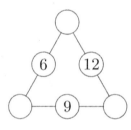

What is this product?

8.3 Practice

Problem 8.11 Write the numbers 23, −13, −4, 5, −10, 11, −1, 20, and 14 in the circles below so that the sum of the numbers inside opposite circles is the same.

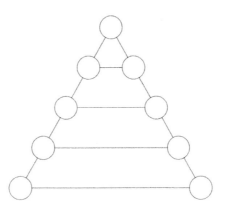

Problem 8.12 Write the numbers 1, . . . , 6 in the circles below, so that the numbers in each side of the triangle add up to 11.

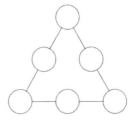

Problem 8.13 Write the numbers 1, 3, 5, 7, 9, 11, 13, 15 and 17 in the circles below so that the sum of the numbers inside opposite circles is the same.

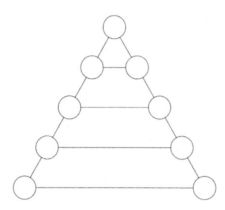

Problem 8.14 Write the numbers 1, ..., 6 in the circles below, so that the numbers in each side of the triangle add up to 12.

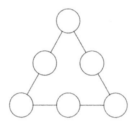

Problem 8.15 Complete the 3×3 magic square with the numbers 5, 10, 15, 20, 25, 30, 35, 40, and 45.

What's the magic sum?

Problem 8.16 Complete the 3×3 magic square with the numbers -8, -6, -4, -2, 0, 2, 4, 6, and 8 .

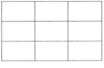

What is the magic sum?

Problem 8.17 Consider the sequence $5, 9, 13, 17, \ldots$. Use the first 9 terms of the sequence to fill in a 3×3 magic square.

What is the magic sum?

Problem 8.18 Complete the 5×5 magic square with the numbers $4, 7, 10, 13, 16, \ldots,$ $73, 76$. What is the magic sum?

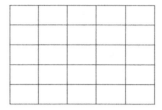

Problem 8.19 Consider the sequence $2, 7, 12, 17, 22, \ldots$. Use the first 25 terms of the sequence to fill in a 5×5 magic square. What is the magic sum?

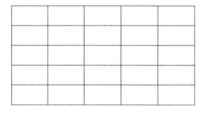

Problem 8.20 Complete the 7×7 magic square with the numbers $-24, -23, -22, \ldots, 21,$ $22, 23, 24$. What is the magic sum?

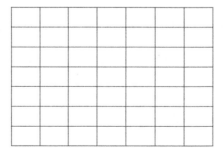

Problem 8.21 Consider the sequence $-48, -46, -44, -42, \ldots$. Use the first 49 terms of the sequence to fill in a 7×7 magic square. What is the magic sum?

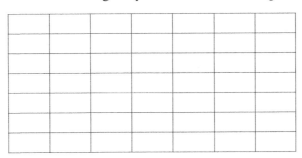

Problem 8.22 Complete the missing numbers in the 4×4 magic square below so that the square is one of the most perfect magic squares. Use the numbers $5, 10, 15, 20, \ldots, 80$. What is the magic sum?

20	75		45
		15	80
	40	65	
70			

Problem 8.23 Complete the missing numbers in the 4×4 magic square below so that the square is one of the most perfect magic squares. Use the numbers $-15, -13, -11, \ldots,$ $11, 13, 15$. What is the magic sum?

1		-13	
13			
-9	-7		

Problem 8.24 Complete the missing numbers in the 4×4 magic square below so that the square is one of the most perfect magic squares. Use the numbers $-21, -15, -9, \ldots,$ $57, 63, 69$. What is the magic sum?

			15
9			
		21	
-3	39		

Problem 8.25 Consider the grid below.

13	16	17	12	19	14
14	17	18	13	20	15
11	14	15	10	17	12
4	7	8	3	10	5
8	11	12	7	14	9
15	18	19	14	21	16

Find 6 numbers on the grid that add up to 78.

Problem 8.26 Fill the 5×5 grid with numbers such that when you pick 5 of them, one from each row and one from each column, their sum is always equal to 100.

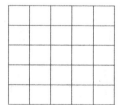

Problem 8.27 Write the numbers 1, 2, 4, 8, 16, 32, 64, 128, and 256 in the circles below so that the product of the numbers inside opposite circles is the same.

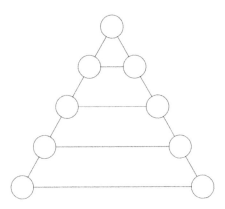

Problem 8.28 Write the numbers $1, 2, 4, 8, 16, 32$ in the circles below so that the product of the numbers in each side of the triangle is equal to 64.

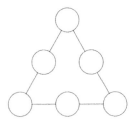

Problem 8.29 Write the numbers 1, 2, 3, 4, 6, 9, 12, 18, and 36 in the circles below so that the product of the numbers inside opposite circles is the same.

Problem 8.30 Write the numbers $1, 2, 4, 8, 16, 32$ in the circles below so that the product of the numbers in each side of the triangle is equal to 128.

Problem 8.31 Write the numbers 1, 3, 5, 9, 15, 25, 45, 75, and 225 in the circles below so that the product of the numbers inside opposite circles is the same.

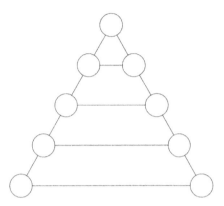

Problem 8.32 Write the numbers $1, 2, 4, 8, 16, 32$ in the circles below so that the product of the numbers in each side of the triangle is equal to 512.

Problem 8.33 Write the numbers $\frac{1}{8}, \frac{1}{4}, \frac{1}{2}, 1, 2, 4$ in the circles below so that the product of the numbers in each side of the triangle is equal to $\frac{1}{2}$.

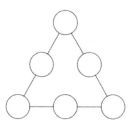

Problem 8.34 Write the numbers $\frac{1}{8}, \frac{1}{4}, \frac{1}{2}, 1, 2, 4$ in the circles below so that the product of the numbers in each side of the triangle is equal to $\frac{1}{4}$.

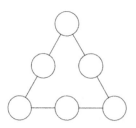

Problem 8.35 Write the numbers $\frac{1}{8}, \frac{1}{4}, \frac{1}{2}, 1, 2, 4$ in the circles below so that the product of the numbers in each side of the triangle is equal to $\frac{1}{8}$.

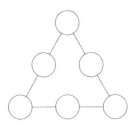

Answer Key to Problems

The answers to the quick response and practice problems in all the chapters are provided here. Only short answers are included. Full solutions for all problems can be found in the solutions manual, *Fun Math Problem Solving for Elementary School Solutions Manual*.

Chapter 1

Problem 1.1 B

Problem 1.2 2310

Problem 1.3 D

Problem 1.4 A

Problem 1.5 6

Problem 1.6 7

Problem 1.7 2

Problem 1.8 C

Problem 1.9 36

Problem 1.10 36

Problem 1.11 25 Prime Chocolates: 2, 3, 5, 7, 11, 13, 17, 19, 23, 29, 31, 37, 41, 43, 47, 53, 59, 61, 67, 71, 73, 79, 83, 89, and 97

Problem 1.12 21 Prime Chocolates with labels 101, 103, 107, 109, 113, 127, 131, 137, 139, 149, 151, 157, 163, 167, 173, 179, 181, 191, 193, 197, and 199

Problem 1.13 5

Problem 1.14 26

Problem 1.15   (a) 10

  (b) 3

  (c) 50

Problem 1.16 Factor trees may vary. Here are three possible factor trees for 120:

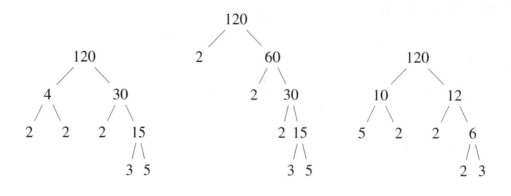

$120 = 2 \times 2 \times 2 \times 3 \times 5$

Problem 1.17 20

Problem 1.18 $2^6 \times 7$

Problem 1.19 15

Problem 1.20 (a) 7

  (b) 50

  (c) 51

Problem 1.21 6

Problem 1.22 72

Problem 1.23 Yes

Problem 1.24 3

Problem 1.25 5 pairs

Problem 1.26 Every 12 weeks

Problem 1.27 9

Problem 1.28 17

Problem 1.29 12

Problem 1.30 (a) $15 = 3 \times 5$; $18 = 2 \times 3 \times 3$; $82 = 2 \times 41$

  (b) 15 has 4 factors, 18 has 6 factors, and 82 has 4 factors

  (c) They have an even number of factors.

Problem 1.31   (a) $16 = 2 \times 2 \times 2 \times 2 \times 2$; $100 = 2 \times 2 \times 5 \times 5$; $121 = 11 \times 11$

(b) 16 has 5 factors, 100 has 9 factors, and 121 has 3 factors

(c) They are all perfect squares and have an odd number of factors.

Problem 1.32 3672

Problem 1.33 210

Problem 1.34 300 inches

Problem 1.35 105

Chapter 2

Problem 2.1 C

Problem 2.2 12

Problem 2.3 B

Problem 2.4 No

Problem 2.5 668

Problem 2.6 0

Problem 2.7 B

Problem 2.8 D

Problem 2.9 A

Problem 2.10 A

Problem 2.11   (a) Yes

  (b) No

  (c) No

Problem 2.12 324 and 432

Problem 2.13   (a) No

  (b) Yes

  (c) Yes

Problem 2.14   (a) No

  (b) Yes

  (c) Yes

Problem 2.15   (a) No

  (b) Yes

  (c) No

Problem 2.16 All

Problem 2.17   (a) Yes

  (b) No

  (c) No

Problem 2.18   (a) 924

  (b) 660, and 924

  (c) 825

Problem 2.19   (a) GCD: 215; LCM: 645

  (b) GCD: 121, LCM: 1210

  (c) 180, 180

Problem 2.20 39 boxes, 10 pencils left over

Problem 2.21 The seagulls and the beach umbrellas

Problem 2.22 The premium tooth brush, and the tooth brush for sensitive teeth.

Problem 2.23 107 stamps in each book, 3 stamps left over

Problem 2.24 332

Problem 2.25

# of boxes	beads per box
3	175
5	105
7	75
15	35

Problem 2.26 5

Problem 2.27 3 pages for 5th grade; 5 pages for 6th grade

Problem 2.28 13 sandwiches

Problem 2.29 The box with 3240 snacks.

Problem 2.30 5

Problem 2.31 (a) Andy

(b) Andy or Dany

(c) Neither

Problem 2.32 3223, 2695, and 4290

Problem 2.33 14

Problem 2.34 (a) Answers may vary. Example answers: 123321, 4994, 13677631

(b) Answers may vary. Example answers: 15851, 363, 48884

(c) Answers may vary. Example answers: 141, 12321, 45754

Problem 2.35 14

Chapter 3

Problem 3.1 A

Problem 3.2 11

Problem 3.3 C

Problem 3.4 15

Problem 3.5 D

Problem 3.6 5

Problem 3.7 3

Problem 3.8 C

Problem 3.9 D

Problem 3.10 B

Problem 3.11 $\dfrac{1}{10}$

Problem 3.12 $\dfrac{5}{8}$

Problem 3.13 $\dfrac{5}{2} = 2\dfrac{1}{2}$ sheets of paper

Problem 3.14   (a) $\dfrac{12}{11}$

   (b) $\dfrac{1}{3}$

   (c) $\dfrac{5}{3}$

Problem 3.15 $\dfrac{2}{5}$

Problem 3.16 Roy. He ate $\dfrac{1}{14}$ of a big bag more than Tracy

Problem 3.17 Brenda: 8; Stacy: 6

Problem 3.18 $\dfrac{17}{30}$

Problem 3.19   (a) Answers may vary. Sample answer: $\dfrac{4}{14}, \dfrac{6}{21}, \dfrac{8}{28}$

   (b) Answers may vary. Sample answer: $\dfrac{1}{4}, \dfrac{2}{8}, \dfrac{3}{12}$

   (c) Answers may vary. Sample answer: $\dfrac{2}{5}, \dfrac{6}{15}, \dfrac{8}{20}$

Problem 3.20 $\dfrac{13}{7} = 1\dfrac{6}{7}$

Problem 3.21 $\dfrac{1}{12}$

Problem 3.22   (a) $\dfrac{19}{16} = 1\dfrac{3}{16}$

   (b) $\dfrac{31}{36}$

   (c) $\dfrac{377}{150} = 2\dfrac{77}{150}$

Problem 3.23   (a) 10

(b) $\dfrac{2}{5}$; 10 pencils

(c) $\dfrac{1}{5}$; 5 pencils

Problem 3.24 $\dfrac{2}{5}$

Problem 3.25   (a) $\dfrac{10}{7}$

(b) $\dfrac{1}{20}$

(c) $\dfrac{1}{8}$

Problem 3.26 $\dfrac{3}{10}$

Problem 3.27   (a) $\dfrac{8}{9}$

(b) $\dfrac{5}{3}$

(c) $\dfrac{16}{27}$

Problem 3.28 50

Problem 3.29 11

Problem 3.30 18

Problem 3.31   (a) $4\dfrac{2}{7}$

(b) $2\dfrac{2}{3}$

(c) $5\dfrac{1}{16}$

Problem 3.32 $\dfrac{34}{3} = 11\dfrac{1}{3}$ liters

Problem 3.33 9 cakes

Problem 3.34 $1100

Problem 3.35 (a) $\dfrac{1}{6}$

(b) $\dfrac{5}{24}$

(c) $\dfrac{39}{40}$

Chapter 4

Problem 4.1 5.43

Problem 4.2 D

Problem 4.3 26.97

Problem 4.4 A

Problem 4.5 C

Problem 4.6 2.4

Problem 4.7 2

Problem 4.8 1.1

Problem 4.9 1.8

Problem 4.10 1.2

Problem 4.11 $0.20

Problem 4.12 $373.98

Problem 4.13 (a) 2 tenths, 20 hundredths, 200 thousandths

(b) 15 tenths, 150 hundredths, 1500 thousandths

(c) 21 tenths, 210 hundredths, 2100 thousandths

Problem 4.14 (a) 54.039

(b) 72.526

(c) 12.001

Problem 4.15 (a) 4, 0, 4

(b) 0, 0, 7

(c) 4, 2. 0

Problem 4.16 (a) 304.028

(b) 4023.408

(c) 356.012

Problem 4.17 3.25 cups

Problem 4.18 (a) 9.75

(b) 0.82

(c) 3.124

Problem 4.19 (a) $\dfrac{237}{100} = 2\dfrac{37}{100}$

(b) $\dfrac{21}{50}$

(c) $3\dfrac{6}{25} = \dfrac{81}{25}$

Problem 4.20   (a) $0.\overline{428571}$

(b) $0.3\overline{72}$

(c) $0.0\overline{21}$

Problem 4.21   (a) $0.\overline{7}, 0.\overline{12}, 0.\overline{123},$

(b) They are all repeating decimals where the numerator of the fraction gives exactly the repeating digits.

(c) $\dfrac{4}{9}, \dfrac{62}{99}, \dfrac{144}{999}$

Problem 4.22   (a) 3.42

(b) 0.28

(c) 8.48

Problem 4.23   (a) 15.413

(b) 12.651

(c) 4.163

Problem 4.24   (a) 5.62

(b) 8.01

(c) 2.55

Problem 4.25 9.9

Problem 4.26   (a) $\dfrac{461}{900}$

(b) $\dfrac{2309}{9900}$

(c) $\dfrac{124613}{9990}$

Problem 4.27 153.53

Problem 4.28   (a) 74.88

(b) 202.77

(c) 144.42

Problem 4.29 1097.46

Problem 4.30   (a) 8.15

  (b) 3.3456

  (c) 0.014664

Problem 4.31   (a) $108

  (b) 144.5

Problem 4.32   (a) 0.04

  (b) 0.036

  (c) 4.6

Problem 4.33 14

Problem 4.34   (a) 320

  (b) 0.6

  (c) $41.\overline{6}$

Problem 4.35 $73.50

Chapter 5

Problem 5.1 D

Problem 5.2 14.5

Problem 5.3 B

Problem 5.4 C

Problem 5.5 160

Problem 5.6 50

Problem 5.7 10

Problem 5.8 20

Problem 5.9 B

Problem 5.10 0.5

Problem 5.11 100 minutes

Problem 5.12 $16

Problem 5.13   (a) 5, 5.4, 5.37
  (b) 124, 124.3, 124.26
  (c) 34, 34, 34.03

Problem 5.14 490

Problem 5.15   (a) 4.2, 4.22, 4.222
  (b) 5.3, 5.28, 5.283
  (c) 6.0, 6.01, 6.008

Problem 5.16   (a) 3780 meters
  (b) 0.4652 meters
  (c) 324.5 meters

Problem 5.17 $320

Problem 5.18   (a) 1.28564 kilometers

(b) 56.928 kilometers

(c) 0.02364 kilometers

Problem 5.19 $100

Problem 5.20   (a) 98.4652 liters

(b) 3640 liters

(c) 6523.5 liters

Problem 5.21   (a) 2.23

(b) $\dfrac{81}{12}$

(c) $4\dfrac{7}{16}$

Problem 5.22 $5.93

Problem 5.23 $100

Problem 5.24   (a) $0.\overline{42}$

(b) $0.\overline{28}$

(c) $\dfrac{12}{33}$

Problem 5.25   (a) 34

(b) 0.1 liters

Problem 5.26 30

Problem 5.27 42 pieces; 0.4 meters left over

Problem 5.28 35

Problem 5.29 $48

Problem 5.30 126

Problem 5.31 200 gallons

Problem 5.32 100

Problem 5.33 1000

Problem 5.34 $70

Problem 5.35 4

Chapter 6

Problem 6.1 C

Problem 6.2 B

Problem 6.3 D

Problem 6.4 14

Problem 6.5 1008

Problem 6.6 3

Problem 6.7 0

Problem 6.8 5

Problem 6.9 6

Problem 6.10 1122

Problem 6.11 7

Problem 6.12 4 or 7

Problem 6.13 (a) 11
(b) 11

Problem 6.14 5

Problem 6.15 27

Problem 6.16 205

Problem 6.17 1036

Problem 6.18 9990

Problem 6.19 5032

Problem 6.20 102375864

Problem 6.21 3

Problem 6.22 370

Problem 6.23 333

Problem 6.24 84

Problem 6.25 8

Problem 6.26 1

Problem 6.27 2222

Problem 6.28 3555

Problem 6.29 22266

Problem 6.30 8

Problem 6.31 1269

Problem 6.32 111555

Problem 6.33 9999555

Problem 6.34 11

Problem 6.35 47847

Chapter 7

Problem 7.1 C

Problem 7.2 71

Problem 7.3 B

Problem 7.4 55

Problem 7.5 53

Problem 7.6 C

Problem 7.7 12

Problem 7.8 7

Problem 7.9 6

Problem 7.10 3

Problem 7.11 2

Problem 7.12 24 flower arrangements; 8 roses left over

Problem 7.13 112

Problem 7.14 720

Problem 7.15 62

Problem 7.16 3171

Problem 7.17 57

Problem 7.18 118

Problem 7.19 53

Problem 7.20 47

Problem 7.21 150

Problem 7.22 98

Problem 7.23 982

Problem 7.24 Sunday

Problem 7.25 Sunday

Problem 7.26 Friday

Problem 7.27 3

Problem 7.28 8:31

Problem 7.29 9:52

Problem 7.30 1:14

Problem 7.31 6

Problem 7.32   (a) 4

  (b) 4

  (c) They are the same

Problem 7.33   (a) 1

  (b) 0

  (c) 2

Problem 7.34   (a) 3

  (b) 3

  (c) 0

Problem 7.35   (a) 3

  (b) 2

  (c) 2

Chapter 8

Problem 8.1 7

Problem 8.2 C

Problem 8.3 96

Problem 8.4 24

Problem 8.5 D

Problem 8.6 D

Problem 8.7 30

Problem 8.8 36

Problem 8.9 4

Problem 8.10 72

Problem 8.11

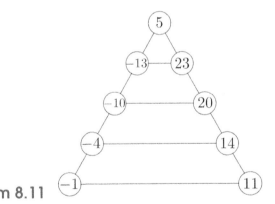

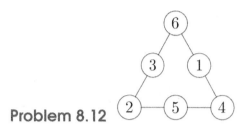

Problem 8.12

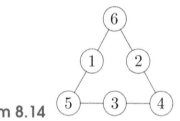

Problem 8.13

Problem 8.14

Problem 8.15 Magic sum: 70

35	5	30
15	25	45
20	40	10

Problem 8.16 Magic sum: 0

−6	8	−2
4	0	−4
2	−8	6

Problem 8.17 Magic sum: 63

33	5	25
13	21	29
17	37	9

Problem 8.18 Magic sum: 200

52	73	4	25	46
70	16	22	43	49
13	19	40	61	67
31	37	58	64	10
34	52	76	7	28

Problem 8.19 Magic sum: 310

82	117	2	37	72
112	22	32	67	77
17	27	62	97	107
47	57	92	102	12
52	87	122	7	42

Problem 8.20 Magic sum: 0

5	14	23	−24	−15	−6	3
13	22	−18	−16	−7	2	4
21	−19	−17	−8	1	10	12
−20	−11	−9	0	9	11	20
−12	−10	−1	8	17	19	−21
−4	−2	7	16	18	−22	−13
−3	6	15	24	−23	−14	−5

Problem 8.21 Magic sum: 0

10	28	46	−48	−30	−12	6
26	44	−36	−32	−14	4	8
42	−38	−34	−16	2	20	24
−40	−22	−18	0	18	22	40
−24	−20	−2	16	34	38	42
−8	−4	14	32	36	−44	−26
−6	12	30	48	−46	−28	−10

Problem 8.22 Magic sum: 170

20	75	**30**	45
25	**50**	15	80
55	40	65	**10**
70	**5**	**60**	35

Problem 8.23 Magic sum: 0

1	**15**	−13	**−3**
−5	**−11**	9	7
13	**3**	**−1**	**−15**
−9	−7	5	11

Problem 8.24 Magic sum: 96

27	**69**	**−15**	15
9	**−9**	**51**	45
63	**33**	21	**−21**
−3	**3**	39	**57**

Problem 8.25 Answers may vary. Pick any six numbers so that you have one from each row and from each column.

Problem 8.26 Answers may vary.

	1	3	5	7	9
11	12	14	16	18	20
13	14	16	18	20	22
15	16	18	20	22	24
17	18	20	22	24	26
19	20	22	24	26	28

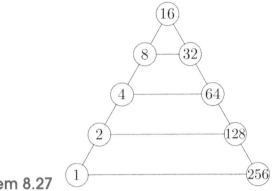

Problem 8.27

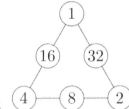

Problem 8.28

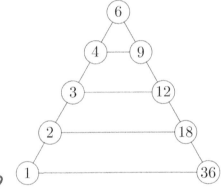

Problem 8.29

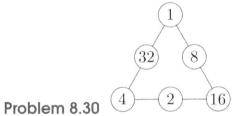

Problem 8.30

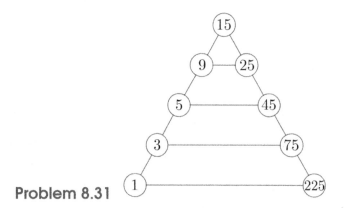

Problem 8.31

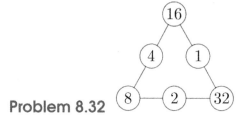

Problem 8.32

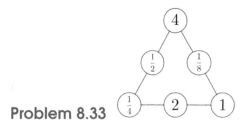

Problem 8.33

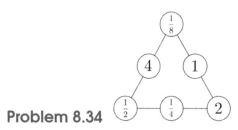

Problem 8.34

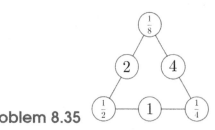

Problem 8.35

Made in the USA
Las Vegas, NV
25 January 2025

16945592R00142